The

MANAGER'S GUIDE TO RESOLVING LEGAL DISPUTES

Also by Jethro K. Lieberman

Business Law and the Legal Environment
  (with George J. Siedel)
The Role of the Courts in American Society *(Editor)*
The Litigious Society
Checks and Balances: The Alaska Pipeline Case
Free Speech, Free Press, and the Law
Crisis at the Bar: Lawyers' Unethical Ethics and What to Do
  About It
Privacy and the Law
Milestones! 200 Years of American Law: Milestones in
  Our Legal History
How the Government Breaks the Law
The Tyranny of the Experts
Are Americans Extinct?
Understanding Our Constitution

The

MANAGER'S GUIDE TO RESOLVING LEGAL DISPUTES

Better Results Without Litigation

James F. Henry & Jethro K. Lieberman

1817

HARPER & ROW, PUBLISHERS, New York
Cambridge, Philadelphia, San Francisco, London
Mexico City, São Paulo, Singapore, Sydney

FIRST EDITION

Library of Congress Cataloging in Publication Data

Henry, James F., 1930–
   The manager's guide to resolving legal disputes.

   (Bibliography: p.
   Includes index.
    1. Dispute resolution (Law)—United States.
  2. Negotiation. I. Lieberman, Jethro Koller.
II. Title.
KF9084.H46   1985   347.73'9   84-48606
ISBN 0-06-015449-7   347.3079

85 86 87 88 89 HC 10 9 8 7 6 5 4 3 2 1

CONTENTS

As a litigant, I should dread a lawsuit beyond almost anything short of sickness and death.

—Learned Hand

A common thread pervades all courtroom contests: Lawyers are natural competitors, and once litigation begins they strive mightily to win using every tactic available. Business executives are also competitors, and when they are in litigation, they often transfer their normal productive and constructive drives into the adversary contest. Commercial litigation takes business executives and their staffs away from the creative paths of development and production and often inflicts more wear and tear on them than the most difficult business problems. . . . The plaintive cry of many frustrated litigants echoes what Learned Hand implied: "There must be a better way."

—Chief Justice Warren E. Burger

As a businessman, if I don't listen to the market, I'm not in business. If I were an attorney, I'd make sure I was involved in alternative dispute resolution, because it may well be the service that the market will demand and I'll have to offer in the future.

—Walter Wriston

The
MANAGER'S GUIDE TO RESOLVING LEGAL DISPUTES

1

TAKING CHARGE
OF YOUR DISPUTES

In 1981, officials at the National Aeronautics and Space Administration had a serious problem. A dispute with Space Communications Company and TRW, Inc., over technical issues in a construction contract signed in 1976 threatened to delay the launch of the Tracking and Data Relay Satellite System, an important component of the space shuttle program. The dispute had been brewing for two years and was about to flare into large-scale litigation. A NASA legal team, wedded to its interpretation of events, was ready to take the depositions of forty people. But the suit would have meant a launch delay of more than one year and would have run up other costs associated with the first TDRSS satellite.

At Spacecom and TRW, executives were no less concerned. During the previous year, their lawyers had spent an estimated $1 million in discovery and depositions, and the lawsuit would have cost at least another million.

Then a lawyer at Mudge Rose Guthrie Alexander & Ferdon, Spacecom's outside New York law firm, suggested a simple solution: a minitrial. Rather than go to court, the parties would lay the case before their own managers, and advance their best arguments within the space of a single day. The managers would then know the strengths of their opponent's case and the weaknesses of their own and be motivated to settle, and settle quickly.

So in February 1982, lawyers for NASA, Spacecom, and TRW sat down to present their case before four people: the director of the Goddard Space Flight Center, NASA's associate administrator for tracking and data systems, Spacecom's president, and a divisional vice-president of TRW. They listened for five hours and met the next day. Within a week they resolved not only the primary dispute, but also several other matters pending before a NASA appeals board.

This speedy, inexpensive settlement of a fractious, costly lawsuit was neither a miracle nor an aberration. It was an example of *alternative dispute resolution* (*ADR*), a movement characterized by *Business Week* and *The New York Times* as a "quiet revolution" in the way corporations and other institutions are learning to settle disputes without resort to the courtroom.

The fundamental lesson of the NASA-TRW settlement is that practical, businesslike methods exist for managers to resolve disputes quickly, effectively, and economically. These methods will work for any manager who is willing to pitch in and become directly involved in the dispute resolution process. The manager who takes charge and maintains control of corporate disputes will discover that it is possible to reduce the large expenses and the days, weeks, or months of precious executive time eaten up by lawsuits. This book will demonstrate the hows and whys of alternative dispute resolution, which we believe to be one of the most promising developments in American business and legal practice in recent years.

Now known by its shorthand name, ADR, alternative dispute resolution is both a philosophy and a set of simple practices that can be powerful tools for a company or an individual caught in the snares of a quarrel that threatens to grow too big to handle, or of a lawsuit that has taken on a life of its own. ADR's fundamental proposition is quite simple: The CEO, manager, and business executive have a strong role to play in devising and executing a settlement strategy. They must learn to use their *business* skills, the skills of negotiation and the art of compromise, to help settle matters that are all too routinely shunted aside to the legal department or an outside lawyer.

As a discipline, ADR is quite new. It was born in the late

1970s and began to gather attention and excitement only in 1981. It did not become widely known within the bar until 1984. So it is a mere infant as these things go.

But its roots are very old, as old as the predilection of almost every litigant to settle the dispute somewhere short of the courtroom steps. ADR takes seriously the statistic which shows, year in and year out, that more than 90 percent of all civil suits are settled before trial. ADR's major theme is this: If a suit is more than likely to be settled eventually, why not settle it early, before the huge costs of discovery and the major expenses of litigation are incurred, before tempers flare out of control, before positions harden to the detriment of all, before a company's business opportunities are squandered, before executives must spend frantic working hours closeted with a lawyer and a stenographer answering questions at a deposition.

One familiar and established form of ADR is *arbitration*, known in general terms to everyone in business. Many industries use arbitration extensively, and labor relations would not work without it. But in the past twenty years or more, many arbitrations have become every bit as complex and costly as litigation. Although it remains a valuable aid to the resolution of business disputes, arbitration, like litigation, has become a last resort.

ADR seeks to go beyond this process in the search for still speedier and less expensive methods that will offer more options for satisfactory resolution of disputes than the win-lose constraints typical of litigation and arbitration. What these methods are and how you can use them make up the bulk of this book.

These methods include the minitrial, which we will describe in some detail. But for all the excitement it has generated, the minitrial is only one of several methods. In the long run, it is likely that *mediation*—a process so far used mainly in labor disputes and domestic relations cases—will be recognized as the sleeping giant of ADR. Most disputes turn on compromisable points, and mediation is ideally designed to foster compromise because it can explore the full range of options open to the disputants.

Still other techniques include the *management* of existing discovery and litigation before it gets to court, *shortcuts* you can use once you are in court, multiparty *collaboration* to establish nonjudicial institutions to resolve disputes that embrace entire industries (as is occurring now in the asbestos lawsuits), more sophisticated and creative uses of *negotiating* (the executive's skill par excellence), and public positions you can take to help foster a climate conducive to the use of ADR by the many rather than the few.

An occasional critic of ADR suggests that dispute resolution outside the courts results in second-class justice. To be sure, an effective lawsuit is more desirable than a failed negotiation, a botched arbitration, or a mediation that leads to further hostilities and no settlement. But the possibility of failure is hardly a reason to forego what promises not second-class justice, but more often justice superior to that achieved by bringing suit. We underscore here that this book is about processes that compare favorably in every way to litigation. This book is designed to show you how you can use these processes to achieve results that far surpass what is possible in the courtroom.

That this can be so is confirmed daily in the international arena. Business executives in Europe, Asia, and elsewhere are understandably wary of making deals with their American counterparts if those deals might land them in American courtrooms. It is no surprise that American-style ADR has awakened international interest: Internationally, ADR (though not by that name) has been practiced for decades, and in some cultures, like those of Japan and China, for centuries. Virtually everything in this book is applicable to the international as well as the domestic arena.

Much of what you are about to read is nothing more than old-fashioned common sense. This ought not to condemn it in the eyes of those who consider themselves sophisticated. Nothing that is complex is worthwhile if it is not anchored in common sense; much that is highly sophisticated can be built on an edifice of common sense. We believe that ADR has struck a chord and is succeeding precisely because it has gone back to basics, has asked some simple questions, and has constructed some new approaches on a widely shared foundation.

In this complex age, we all can use a few simplicities that work.

2

THE PATHOLOGY OF LITIGATION

Every year, Americans take their grievances and quarrels to court in record numbers. In the 1980s, the statistics show that annually more than 11 million civil complaints arrive in the major state trial courts of the nation (and nearly a quarter of a million suits in the federal courts). Most of these suits, it is true, do not get very far. About 94 percent are dropped or settled—through the negotiations of lawyers—long before they get to trial.

But do not be misled. That leaves more than 600,000 state suits and some 20,000 federal suits every year that march on through the judicial process to verdicts. These trials, as any business executive who has been involved in one will testify, are costly, time-consuming, and exhausting—and often only a prelude to years of equally costly, time-consuming, and exhausting appeals.

This was not always so. It was the rare case forty years ago, or even twenty-five years ago, that disrupted the office, took executives away from their desks, cost the company hundreds of thousands (if not millions) of dollars in lawyers' fees, and put the business at risk of losing even more in a jury damage award. Since the 1950s, *litigation*—the process of suing—has developed pathological tendencies.

The pathology of litigation can be viewed from many perspectives: (1) how social, economic, and technological changes have motivated more and more people to sue; (2) how the dynamics of a particular dispute lead the parties to court; and (3) how the system leads lawyers to prolong cases.

Social, Economic, and
Technological Changes

No one can doubt that during the past forty years our society has become vastly more complex and interdependent. We have more and better technologies: in transportation and communication, in wonder drugs and chemicals—in all the developments of the modern age. But technology has side effects, and large numbers of people are injured in ways that were not possible before—witness the major toxic tort suits (like asbestos and Agent Orange) filed in recent days.

Moreover, people are far more aware of their rights than ever before, and—largely because of new law and judicial interpretations—have far more rights to claim than at the end of World War II. These rights are political (civil rights, equality of opportunity), social (entitlement programs), and economic (rights to recover for an endless stream of potential damages).

With these rights has come an awareness of how to enforce them. No group has failed to learn the lessons of our litigious society: that significant gains can be won in court, even if significant social costs are incurred. In the field of product liability, for example, the courts have virtually remade the law, so that all across the country people sue manufacturers who only a quarter-century ago would have faced no liability at all. Business enterprises, too, have learned this lesson. In the 1950s, few companies sued each other; difficulties were either ignored or negotiated. But some time in the 1960s, business enterprises began to take to the courts an increasing variety of commercial, financial, antitrust, and other types of legal claims.

The growth in lawsuits has been affected by lawyers' fee practices. The *contingent fee*—the client owes the lawyer nothing unless the lawyer wins the case—has had a major impact on the types and growth of tort cases like product liability and toxic substances suits. (And in many other types of cases, like those involving antitrust and certain environmental claims, lawyers are permitted by statute to collect their fee from a losing defendant, thus prompting many to sue who might otherwise have stayed out of court.) If the contingent fee practice has prompted lawsuits, the defense bar's fee structure does nothing to end these suits quickly. For most law firms today charge on a cost-plus basis, with all the incentives such a system provides for prolonging the work. Thus fees come less to reward accomplishment than to recompense the legal staff for the number of hours spent on the case.

The Dynamics of Particular Disputes

These social and technological revolutions have led many to file lawsuits. But the changes do not, by themselves, explain why the disputes are not resolved through negotiation. To understand this, it is necessary to examine the particular dynamics of legal disputes.

In a competitive society such as ours, disputes are to be expected as a normal part of the landscape. The trouble arises when the dispute passes out of the hands of the disputants themselves and into the hands of the lawyers. This creates a kind of chain reaction, a momentum that can actually run counter to the disputants' aims.

First, those with the most direct stake in resolving the dispute are now removed from immediate responsibility to attempt to do so. New sets of people, with different incentives, suddenly become involved. In large business lawsuits, the massive egos of certain leading litigators do not predispose them to quick settlement. They relish the chance to compete in this arena. Indeed, the litigator's approach—akin to legal warfare—itself tends to heat up the dispute's emotional intensity. All disputes have emotional overtones, but when the litigator takes hold, the emotional pitch of the dispute rises yet another notch, actually making it more difficult to settle.

Second, this characteristic approach of the lawyer has a resonant effect on the client. Seeing their lawyers charged up with energy to go after the "enemy," many clients begin to believe that the other disputant really is an enemy, with all that that term connotes. So the possibility of settlement becomes even more remote.

Third, once the lawyer assumes responsibility for the case, the chance of a communication breakdown increases dramatically. A manager who knows his business well may not be equipped to teach his counsel all the nuances. Indeed, in a complex enterprise, it is probably impossible even for the most sophisticated managers to do so truly adequately. So the lawyer will proceed with one set of assumptions, giving the client a position that is not what the client himself might have chosen.

Fourth, the lawyers' code of professional responsibility forbids the lawyer for one side to talk directly to the client on the other side. All communication must be done through the lawyers. Filtered through two sets of lawyers, the information necessary to settlement becomes distorted, as anyone who has ever played the children's game of "telephone" can attest.

Finally, the manifold aggravations of the legal process lead most busy managers to wash their hands of the entire proceeding. Solving disputes does not look like the kind of thing that managers are hired to do; dispute resolution is commonly thought of as "unproductive." In any event, the sheer effort and time that most lawsuits take force the manager to leave the disputing, and hence the settlement effort, to the lawyers.

The System's Impact on Prolonging the Case

The factors discussed above do not altogether explain why lawsuits take so long once they get there. To understand that, we must look at our whole system of jurisprudence, which is rooted in the *adversary system*. All litigants—including the corporate litigant—are entitled to counsel of their choice. The lawyers a client chooses are bound by a formal code of ethics, part of a deeply felt tradition, to represent the client *zealously*, to work in the client's behalf to the outermost bounds of the law.

The adversary system puts the lawyer's fidelity to client ahead of country or common humanity, but this is not, in itself, the cause of our dissatisfaction with litigation as it is practiced today. For the adversary system has always been part of our legal process, and the current level of dissatisfaction with litigation is relatively new. Moreover, the adversary system is culturally linked to our competitive ethos. A market economy that encourages individuals to compete requires a legal system that gives clients fiercely independent lawyers ready to do battle against the adversary.

However, major elements of the adversary legal system have changed dramatically during the past four decades. One such change was a seemingly beneficial revision, some forty-five years ago, in the procedural rules. Another has been the growth of major law firms. Still others are the spread of legal education, the complexities of the law from the 1960s on, and the needs of business. How does all this connect?

In 1938, the United States Supreme Court adopted rules intended to abolish the "Perry Mason" use of surprise witnesses and evidence in court. The new rules modernized the practice of what, in legal parlance, is called *discovery*. They give broad power to each side to probe, before trial, the adversary's strengths and weaknesses by sifting through the actual evidence—both documentary and testimonial—that will be produced in court. The basis for the rules, imitated in time by the courts in most states, is that the old "sporting theory" of justice is unjust: A litigant's case should not stand or fall on whether the lawyer happens to ferret out the evidence. A trial should be a search for truth, and the system should encourage lawyers to take whatever steps are necessary before trial to ensure that the full record will be paraded before judge and jury. The rules thus substituted a pretrial fact-finding process for what had previously been a haphazard courtroom game.

Discovery comes in three major forms. One type is documentary evidence. A simple written request to the adversary for, say, "any documents concerning the sale of preferred shares during the period 1980–1984" is legally sufficient, and unless some special privilege applies, the party to whom the request is made must turn over what could amount to thousands or even millions of pieces of paper.

The Litton-AT&T case shows just how expensive discovery can be. In 1976, Litton Industries filed an antitrust suit against American Telephone & Telegraph Company. In response to an AT&T discovery request, Litton delivered 3 million documents to its Sunnyvale, California, offices. For seven months in 1977, an AT&T team of 69 lawyers, paralegals, clerks, and microfilm technicians worked 2,910 hours to find and copy 1.8 million documents relevant to the defense. The estimated cost of this search was $532,000, of which $156,000 was paid for microfilming. This is a typical document search in a large antitrust case.

A second type of discovery is oral testimony, made by way of deposition. Again, a simple request to a company that the opposing lawyers intend to "depose" the CEO and others is enough to start the process. The depositions are taken outside the court, usually in the lawyer's office, and can go on for days and sometimes weeks.

A third type of discovery is deposition by written interrogatory: Lengthy sets of written questions are presented and detailed answers are demanded. The answers frequently serve as the basis for requests to discover documentary evidence and to take depositions.

To ensure that the courts would observe the spirit of the new rules and not interpret their mandate narrowly, the Supreme Court made it clear that documents and oral testimony are discoverable *whether or not admissible in court*. As long as it might lead to admissible evidence, documents must be made available to the opposing attorney, and officers and employees must submit to questioning when properly requested.

That is a striking rule, for it means that *virtually anything* is discoverable: from an entire warehouse full of documents to the recollections of the CEO and all the corporate managers below him.

Indeed, so striking is this rule that its full implications were not realized for many years. Not until the late 1950s and early 1960s did it become apparent—as companies began to sue each other more frequently under antitrust laws, and consumers began to sue under a variety of federal laws—that *a lawyer could file a suit without having any theory of the case to begin with.* That is, it would be enough simply to charge that company X had violated the Sherman Act without specifying exactly how. Once the suit was filed—simple enough to do at the cost of a few dollars—the plaintiff's lawyers could rummage through company X's files for evidence of wrongdoing, to see whether there was any evidence to make out some charge or other (and without much fear of being penalized if they found none).

Now although the possibility of conducting such a "fishing expedition" has existed since 1938, it was not until recently a practical possibility. Extended discovery is difficult, time-consuming, and frequently exhausting work. A solo practitioner or a small partnership, with hundreds of matters in the office to work on—wills, house closings, divorce settlements, and the like—would not be able to conduct the kind of widespread discovery with which we are familiar today. Only when law offices reached a certain size, so that a dozen or more lawyers could work on a single case month after month, would that kind of discovery become practicable. And not until in the 1960s these law offices became numerous enough did the social impact of this kind of discovery practice make itself felt.

Commenting on this vast growth in discovery, U.S. Supreme Court Justice Lewis F. Powell has said: "Litigation costs have become intolerable, and they cast a lengthening shadow over the basic fairness of our legal system." Walter Wriston, former CEO of Citibank, agrees. At a 1984 conference on management's expectation of counsel in the 1980s, he warned that lawyers "should ignore at their peril the problems of the existing discovery process. The economics of it raises serious questions of the entire justice system."

Private practitioners were not alone in contributing to this problem. During the 1970s, law schools rapidly increased in number and by the 1980s turned out more than three times as many lawyers as they had in the 1960s (some 35,000 law students now graduate annually, compared to the 10,000 who took the bar examination in the mid-1960s). The change was not merely in numbers, however. Competitive pressures forced most schools to become far more professional and rigorous than they had been. Reflecting the changes in legal practice, the courses in procedure and related subjects made it clear to students that the days of seat-of-the-pants trial work were over.

Students began to learn in schools the bywords that would be instilled in them when they came to work for a firm: *Leave no stone unturned.* It is unprofessional to "wing it," to interview the client and rely on one's wits to prevail before the jury. From now on, it would be necessary to look under every rock for every worm that might be wriggling, to use the metaphor of Weyman I. Lundquist, a San Francisco lawyer who takes a dim view of the excesses of the discovery system. He sees the law schools "following the law firms' lead by turning out mechanics rather than artisans."

Leaving no stone unturned is the equivalent to "risk no surprises in court." If there is an extra file to be looked at, look at it. If there is an extra potential witness to talk to, talk to her. If there are more questions to be asked, ask them. Lawyers "assume it is professionally irresponsible to fight the war without making a full commitment to maneuvering for whatever advantages might be available," says Wayne D. Brazil, a U.S. magistrate in San Francisco.

To Lundquist and other lawyers who deplore the spread of this philosophy, the day of the *trial lawyer* has ended; it is the time of the *litigator*. As Lundquist puts it:

> Litigators march forth from law firms flanked by junior partners, associates, and paralegals much as fifteenth-century Italian armies ventured from warring city-states. These armies left home and lived well off the land as they proceeded towards the enemy. They avoided direct combat at all costs. The process leading to it was too rewarding, while battle itself was too risky. Thus does litigation proceed today.

Lest the business executive become smug—and angrier than warranted—it is important to note that the transition from trial lawyer to litigator, and the excesses that are associated with it, were not simple promptings of lawyers' lust for money. None of this would have come about but for the complexities of the law and the active complicity of corporate clients.

The law's complexities had their roots in the New Deal: The new securities laws, other regulatory schemes, and the increased emphasis on antitrust prosecutions spelled a new legal environment for business. Proving a case based on complicated federal statutes and defending against one are large undertakings. Moreover, business itself has grown more complex; contracts that were once relatively simple affairs now run into the hundreds of pages, so that even cases based on commercial dealings between companies can call for voluminous evidence.

An occasional case against business filed by the government might have been tolerable, but by the early 1960s, businesses began to sue each other. Perhaps the wave of intercorporate suits stemmed from the federal antitrust prosecution of General Electric for price fixing: Several thousand private suits were filed in the wake of the Justice Department's successful prosecution of GE, in which several of its executives went to jail. Whatever the cause, it became clear by the 1970s that corporations themselves are major generators of suits against business.

The seventies also taught activists the power of litigation. The wave of new federal and state laws made it easier to file suits, easier for consumers, suppliers, governments, and others with grievances against the business community. Employment disputes, environmental actions, and consumer complaints joined the antitrust, stockholders', and general commercial lawsuits that assaulted the business corporation (and other institutions) from the late 1960s on.

In both the prosecution and defense of these suits, corporations encouraged their lawyers to hone the discovery weapon. Corporations did this in several ways. First, and perhaps most important, they turned over the entire legal matter, strategy and all, to the lawyers. Until the late 1970s, this habit usually meant sending the case to an outside law firm. But companies did so with the admonition to *leave no stone unturned.* And if they did not say so in so many words, it was clearly understood that this was the governing rule. Without being aware that they were doing so, the CEO and senior management were dictating a major strategy without necessarily thinking through the consequences: a duel to the death, or at least to serious bloodletting of the corporate treasury, of executive time and talent, and to lost opportunity costs.

This is an important point, so let us underscore it. During the 1970s, one of us had occasion to lunch with the chairman and CEO of one of America's ten largest manufacturing corporations, a company then involved in multibillion-dollar litigation. The chairman was visibly annoyed with the conduct of lawyers and the legal system and pounded the table in anger at the waste and the time-consuming, "dilly-dallying, shilly-shallying" tactics in which they seemed to engage on behalf of his company. The lawyers take forever, he complained, and their monthly bills mount up to astronomical amounts. (His complaint recalled the celebrated quip attributed to Frank Cary, then chairman of IBM, that his law department had an unlimited annual budget, "and every year they exceed it.")

Finally, the CEO calmed down enough to allow a question: Was he saying that his lawyers did all that he complained about without any direction from his company? Wasn't it possible that they were acting as they did because the client—the corporation—had somehow communicated to them the need to "go all the way," to press the opposition to the wall, to *leave no stone unturned?* A curious expression clouded his face, as he obviously reflected on meetings he must have had with his general counsel. Sheepishly, he admitted that he had told his in-house lawyers exactly that, and with that admission he changed the subject.

Nor is discovery practice limited to a plaintiff's offense. Sophisticated firms and companies have learned to use discovery defensively as well, to turn it to their advantage by delaying a case that they would prefer never to come to trial. If most law firms and corporations do not deliberately and willfully abuse the discovery system, nevertheless the potential for delay is always present. In 1978, Sante Fe County (NM) Judge Edwin L. Felter imposed the largest discovery sanction in history. Midway through, he stopped a trial by United Nuclear Corporation against General Atomic Company involving uranium supply contracts and awarded United Nuclear $8.5 million in cash and the rights to almost $1 billion worth of uranium, because of General Atomic's two-year-long "obstruction of justice and . . . a willful, deliberate, and flagrant scheme of delay, resistance, obfuscation and evasion in discovery matters." General Atomic had resisted turning over documents tending to show it had been a member of a uranium cartel, resisted so hard, in fact, that it transferred most of the documents to Canada, which has a law barring dissemination to U.S. litigants of any information contained in documents stored in Canada and concerning the cartel.

Despite these risks, litigators continue to press the discovery system to the limits. Says Peter Gruenberger, head of an American Bar Association committee on discovery abuse: "There is an imagined need to take every deposition, to ask for every document, and to propound every interrogatory. And the other side frequently feels the need to resist to the end, until it is their turn to do the same." Today, virtually every litigator, whether acting for plaintiff or defendant, will tell you that he or she dare not suggest to a client doing anything other than serving as a gladiator of old, to do all-out battle against the enemy. To do anything less, to suggest that the client simmer down at the beginning and think of some nonlitigious way to solve the problem, is to risk seeming "weak." This is not a theoretical concern: It is the very real and very practical concern of some seasoned litigators, who at private meetings devoted to discussing alternatives to litigation admit to being anguished over their frequent inability to talk sense into clients.

Does that mean that nothing can be done to fight the pathology of litigation? We do not believe that the situation is hopeless. On the contrary, the situation seems full of hope if those involved in litigation will recognize that the solution is not necessarily to change the rules of the legal system, but to use the rules to the client's advantage. This will require that the client not be reactive, but "proactive." It will require that the corporation no longer delegate every aspect of the case to the lawyers, but take charge of significant aspects of legal matters that affect its operations. It will require the client to assume responsibility for determining how many risks to take, to walk away from the comfortable rule of leaving no stone unturned and to calculate when certain stones should be left in place, uninspected. It will require an understanding that "tough" lawyers are not the only or always the best kinds of lawyers, and that lawyers who want to settle creatively are not always "weak." Lawyers with alternative solutions to complex problems should be listened to, even eagerly. Finally, overcoming the pathology of litigation will require the client to work with the lawyers to craft a *business* approach to legal problems.

To just such an approach, applicable to many business disputes, we now turn.

3

TRW v. TELECREDIT: THE FIRST MINITRIAL

Telecredit, Inc., was a small company holding patents on several computerized devices that allow department stores and other users to verify a customer's creditworthiness and his right to use the credit cards presented for purchases. The company had annual sales of about $8 million. Telecredit had licensed several manufacturers to produce the patented devices, but none of the patents had even been "tested" in litigation. Such testing is an important consideration to any patent holder, because the courts upset a significant percentage of patents awarded by the U.S. Patent and Trademark Office.

Telecredit came to the conclusion that giant TRW, Inc., was infringing its patents on computerized credit-card and check-authorization machines that TRW manufactured. In late 1974, Telecredit sued. It sought $6 million in damages and an injunction against further infringement. An injunction would have effectively put an end to one of TRW's major product lines.

TRW denied the infringement. Moreover, it asserted that Telecredit's patents were legally invalid, a claim which, if upheld, would have permitted anyone to use Telecredit's inventions, thus destroying much of the company's assets.

For two years, the company lawyers went about gathering up corporate documents. Both technical and business employees of each company had competed directly for years, and as the case progressed, the managers in both companies grew heated. "The feelings between the two companies and even the lawyers were extremely negative," Lee A. Ault III, Telecredit president and CEO, later recalled. Perhaps the major reason for the hard feelings was the absolute belief by each side that it was right and that the adversary therefore must have been acting in bad faith.

The emotional climate of the proceedings was not aided by the pace of discovery. Telecredit began to inspect tens of thousands of documents and to depose numerous TRW employees. (By 1977, some 100,000 documents had changed hands.) Telecredit lawyers also sent multiple sets of interrogatories, demanding innumerable answers. The lawyers also demanded that TRW admit certain facts, on pain of paying for Telecredit's efforts to prove the facts at trial if TRW refused to admit them beforehand (a procedure known as *request for admission* and allowed under the Federal Rules of Civil Procedure). TRW too pushed forward with a massive discovery program aimed at uncovering evidence that would show Telecredit's patents to be invalid.

This pretrial maneuvering went on for thirty months, without a trial or even pretrial conference date set. (In part, the delay was attributable to the illness of the judge, although it is not uncommon these days in complex cases for trial dates to be set more than three years down the road.) During this time, the parties made sporadic efforts to discuss settlement, but every time the lawyers got together, the discussions fell apart over the issue of the good faith or bad faith of the adversaries. Telecredit remained convinced that TRW was willfully appropriating its inventions and that its asking price, $6 million, was not excessive in that light. TRW thought the figure was wildly inflated, even if it turned out that it was in some way infringing.

TRW had repeatedly demanded that Telecredit demonstrate how the TRW machines infringed the patents. "We wanted a showing," said one of TRW's lawyers. Finally, Telecredit asked TRW whom it would believe if such a showing were made.

Faced with the prospect of still more depositions of inventors and technical personnel and with the continuing uncertainty that kept both companies' business plans in check, the parties began to discuss the possibility of resolving the case outside the courtroom. At first, Telecredit proposed arbitration, the traditional noncourtroom procedure for resolving legal disputes (see Chapter 8). But TRW balked, for a number of reasons: At the time it was not clear whether a patent dispute could legally be arbitrated, and TRW in any event was worried about the conventional wisdom that arbitrators tend to "split the baby in half," which even at that would work out to be a sizable bill.

So TRW lawyers began to negotiate with Telecredit cofounder (and nonlawyer) Ronald A. Katz, then serving as the company's patent licensing administrator, for a procedure that would lead to a settlement. After several weeks, they hammered out a strategy they called an "information exchange." The parties agreed to adhere to a rigorous six-week schedule for limited discovery of certain documents not yet in their possession and for exchanging briefs and position papers. (All pending discovery in the lawsuit would be suspended.) At the end of the six weeks, they would present their evidence and arguments orally to top management representatives of each company.

Unlike a conventional trial, in which lawyers have a tendency to explore all the byways of a case, the information exchange would necessitate the parties' presenting their "best case," because each would have only four hours to make the presentations (if the case had gone to trial, it might have consumed weeks of court time). Following the presentations and rebuttals on the second day, the senior managers to whom the case was to be presented were obligated to meet privately and attempt to settle the case—by themselves, without lawyers being present.

The information exchange was to be moderated by a "neutral advisor." However, the parties would not be trying the case to him as if he were a judge; he would preside to preserve order. He would have no authority to push for a compromise. Only if the parties failed to reach agreement would he have a substantive role. If the managers failed to settle during their private discussions, the neutral advisor was bound to give the parties a written, nonbinding opinion detailing his perception of the strengths and weaknesses of each party's case and predicting how the case would end if taken to court. The managers would then meet again to see whether the neutral advisor's opinion had made them more amenable to settlement. (To preserve confidentiality, the companies agreed that the neutral's opinion could never be used for any purpose beyond the one contemplated in the information exchange. Specifically, the opinion could not be used in court if the parties wound up there. Nor could the neutral advisor ever again serve as a trial witness, consultant, or expert for either party.)

Adopting an eight-page set of rules that called for the information exchange to be conducted in utmost secrecy, Telecredit and TRW were on the verge of making legal history.

On July 20, 1977, the parties met around an oversized table in a cramped room at the Century Plaza Hotel in Los Angeles. Present for Telecredit was CEO Ault. Attending for TRW was Vice-President Richard A. Campbell. Both had authority to settle the case without returning to headquarters for instructions or ratification. The neutral advisor was James F. Davis, formerly a U.S. Court of Claims trial judge with considerable patent law expertise and now a partner in the Washington law firm of Howrey & Simon.

That afternoon, for four hours, Telecredit's attorneys presented to Campbell, Ault, and Davis its *prima facie* case for infringement. Under the agreed rules, all exhibits and introductory briefs had already been given to Davis, who had the authority to put written questions to the parties' expert witnesses before the information exchange.

The next morning, July 21, TRW had ninety minutes to reply to Telecredit's main case, with thirty more minutes allocated to Telecredit to rebut. The third hour of the morning was reserved for an open question-and-answer session involving all aspects of the infringement claim. The same sequence began again that afternoon, beginning with TRW's four-hour presentation of its patent invalidity claims, followed the next morning by Telecredit's reply, TRW's rebuttal, and the Q & A session.

The principal speakers during these twelve hours of presentation, reply, and rebuttal were the parties' lawyers. But each had testimony from expert witnesses, in both cases an authority on computers. Also testifying for Telecredit was a licensee's former employee. TRW had a scientist present certain technical matters.

After each segment of the proceedings, neutral advisor Davis summed up the case as it then stood. This gave the parties immediate feedback, allowing them to size up how their presentations were "coming across."

The effect of the presentations is described well by TRW's attorneys in an article published later:

> During the presentations each side gained significant new insights into the opposing party's claims. For example, plaintiff [Telecredit] presented a new argument during its initial four-hour presentation which it felt anticipated and answered one of defendant's most important invalidity theories. Although defendant [TRW] had been aware that plaintiff might eventually take such a position, plaintiff's discovery responses, up to the point of the Information Exchange, seemed to defendant to indicate otherwise. Plaintiff's presentation on this issue required defendant's attorneys to reevaluate a key element of their defense and to restructure significantly their planned presentation for the next day. After an all-night blitz, defense counsel presented a response to plaintiff's new argument that, for the first time in the litigation, sharply pinpointed the parties' precise legal and factual differences on a vital element of the case. Additional discussion and questions from management and the advisor exposed difficulties for

plaintiff that prior thereto it had not clearly discerned. Similarly, plaintiff made several other points during its initial presentation and during its rebuttal to defendant's presentation that enabled defendant to appreciate more fully plaintiff's position.

The fourteen hours at the Century Plaza were not emotion-free. The tension was palpable, and tempers sometimes flared. But neutral advisor Davis kept the proceedings going, insisting that the parties get down to business and stick to the schedule. Immediately after the final Q & A session, Davis gave his preliminary view on all the issues. He subsequently has written that he believes these would have been his final views had he been required to write an advisory opinion. As it turned out, he did not have to.

Ault and Campbell went off by themselves to another room, where they talked about how the case might be resolved. It was here that the minitrial proved its worth, for the hearings gave the executives a basis on which to negotiate: Despite the emotional overtones of the case and the time that had already been consumed in litigation, they reached a working agreement within *thirty minutes*. The actual formal agreement took several more weeks to iron out, with lawyers participating, but its essence was struck in that thirty-minute talk between Ault and Campbell. (In essence, the agreement called for TRW to pay for a license against credits that Telecredit would grant, assuming the Patent Office would issue Telecredit new patents, which the Patent Office eventually did.)

The total elapsed time from the moment when the parties first began to discuss the concept of an information exchange to the day when they signed the formal agreement ending the litigation was ninety days. Ault estimated that the savings in lawyers' fees alone was $1 million.

Suppose the information exchange had not worked? After all, it was not binding, and the parties were under no legal compulsion to settle. Wouldn't the exchange then have been a waste of time and money? No one associated with the process thought so. Virtually everything done to prepare for the exchange of information would have had to be done eventually; in fact, going through the process would undoubtedly have helped the lawyers sharpen their trial strategy.

Moreover, most of the costs incurred in preparing for the two-day hearings would have had to be borne anyway. The only costs that would not have been duplicated were the costs of negotiating the agreement to hold the exchange and the parties' time during the two-day hearings. For one of the parties, these costs amounted to only one-quarter of the cost of the information exchange itself. Although the costs of the first minitrial have never been published, knowledgeable observers suggest that they could not have amounted to more than $25,000.

Why the information exchange works we reserve for the next chapter. But the lesson is clear. Said Ron Katz: "We have to remove lawyers from their pugilistic environment and bring in the problem-solving abilities of businessmen."

The parties called their invention an "information exchange." Today, however, no one uses that term. The process has come to be known instead as a "minitrial." The name came from a headline writer. A year after Telecredit v. TRW was settled, some of the attorneys involved in the case appeared on a panel discussing new approaches to dispute resolution. The panel was part of the American Bar Association's centennial meeting held in August 1978 in New York City. Several reporters were present, including one from *The New York Times*. The next day, the *Times* account ran under a headline proclaiming that a "minitrial" held the secret to inexpensive resolution of business disputes. The name was made up out of whole cloth, but it stuck.

Minitrial it is.

4

WHY IT WORKS:
THE COMMON ELEMENTS
OF A MINITRIAL

Because the minitrial is a voluntary method of resolving business disputes, its form is flexible. One of its virtues is that it may be tailored to the specific requirements of the dispute, the companies, and the personalities of the executives and lawyers involved. Nevertheless, most minitrials succeed because they have incorporated certain procedures into the ground rules drawn up by the parties.

Negotiate the Ground Rules

Since minitrials are voluntary, the parties must agree not only to conduct one, but to provide for a set of ground rules or common procedures, often known as the "protocol," to guide the participants before and during the minitrial itself.

One set of model rules is given in Appendix A. But the precise rules are less important than the process of arriving at them. The key is to persuade your adversary to accept the process—letting key executives with authority to settle listen to a highly abbreviated version of both sides of the case—and then to agree with that adversary on the procedures that will best achieve your mutual goal of settlement.

You can initiate the idea of the minitrial through your lawyer, through principals in the company, or through a neutral intermediary. How best to proceed depends on the stage of the dispute and its circumstances; no rule of thumb is possible. If the dispute has not yet gone to lawyers, you might want to call your opposite number directly and suggest that you talk settlement through a nonbinding, focused procedure. If the case is in litigation, your lawyer would normally raise the possibility with the opposing attorney. But you might want to consider having a neutral third person sound out your adversary about the prospect for serious settlement talks. Why use a neutral to sound out your adversary? The short and complete answer is that you will necessarily be the worst salesperson to call on your adversary with an offer to sell a speedy resolution. This third person can be someone known to and respected by both parties, or a professional dispute resolver hired to bring the parties together. (For more information on where to secure such neutrals, see Chapter 10.)

The initial contact should be informal. You do not want to hand over a detailed blueprint at the outset; instead you should relay your willingness to enter into a structured but largely informal settlement discussion. That is because the process of determining the details of the minitrial blueprint will help bring the parties closer together. It emphasizes points of agreement rather than points of difference on which litigation is focused. Negotiating the blueprint replaces a contentious state of mind with a cooperative state of mind, one conducive to agreement. It does this by focusing on procedures, where emotions are far less likely to hold sway, rather than on the substance that has provoked the controversy. Through their discussions, the lawyers—and to a degree the business principals—will have an opportunity to develop a sense of mutual trust, as they seek through the give-and-take of talks a set of rules that will be of mutual benefit.

The minitrial protocol should address at least eleven concerns:

1. *The issues to be discussed.* Although the nonbinding status of the minitrial means that you need not be concerned about rigidly enforcing restrictions on certain issues, it makes sense to have at least a general idea about which issues are to be discussed and which are out of bounds.

2. *The amount of allowable discovery.* In the usual case, discovery will be relatively limited. If the parties are in the midst of litigation, much discovery will have already taken place anyway.

3. *Obligations to present and negotiate.* The protocol should obligate the parties to present their best cases and to negotiate following the presentation of evidence.

4. *Persons to be present.* The names of the business principals to be present, the number of lawyers, experts, and other witnesses should be aired and agreed upon at this time. Most important, the protocol should set forth the status of the business representatives and state their authority to settle.

5. *Time, place, and schedule.* The ground rules should set forth the date, time, and place of the minitrial. It should also provide a schedule of events—how much time to be allocated to the parties' direct case, to rebuttal, to questions, and so on.

6. *Rules of evidence.* No formal rules of evidence are required, but if certain rules are to be followed (for example, no expert testimony except from experts actually present at the hearing), these should be stated formally in the protocol.

7. *Exchange of briefs and other documents.* It may make sense for the parties to exchange briefs and other documents in advance of the minitrial. Again, these should be specified in the protocol, along with the timetable for their submission.

8. *Neutral advisor.* You will certainly wish to agree on whether to use a neutral advisor and if so, how he or she will be selected. When selected, the neutral advisor's name should be incorporated in the protocol.

9. *Confidentiality.* The protocol should provide for the confidentiality of all documents exchanged and statements made, and for their inadmissibility (and the inadmissibility of any opinion given by the neutral advisor) in any future proceeding. Note that there are two types of confidentiality to be concerned about. The first concern is to prevent the information divulged in the proceedings from subsequent disclosure at

trial. The second concern is to keep all news of the proceeding private, so that the dispute is not aired in public (that is, in the press).

10. *Apportionment of costs.* You should agree at the outset on how costs of the witnesses, neutral advisor, and any others should be apportioned. It is generally the rule that the neutral advisor's fee is divided evenly between the parties.

11. *Pending litigation.* Finally, you will want to agree on how to handle any litigation that is currently pending. Usually, the parties agree to suspend discovery and to stay the litigation until the minitrial is complete and they have had some period of time to negotiate a settlement.

Limit the Time to Prepare

One of the most important factors in the success of minitrials to date has been the limited amount of time that the lawyers and others have been allowed for preparation. Ordinarily, much of the time devoted to pretrial discovery in formal litigation is relatively unfocused. It is a cross between a fishing expedition (hoping to catch particularly important documents) and a dredging of the lake bed (searching for everything). As the lawyers go about this task, they do not necessarily concentrate on which documents and depositions are key. However, when the lawyers are suddenly faced with an extremely short period of time—perhaps six weeks to two months—in which to prepare the case as a whole, they and everyone else connected with the case suddenly focus on the heart of the matter. Thus this short period is crucial, because it forces everyone to do what ideally they should have done from the outset. It eliminates the inconsequential, puts the case in perspective, and short-circuits the expensive routines the lawyers had been or would be pursuing.

Preparation time must necessarily include briefing the key executives who will be present for each party. No business representative should walk into the minitrial cold, without understanding the basics of the case, the nature of the minitrial process, or what is expected once the presentations are completed.

Abbreviate the Hearing

The minitrial itself should be confined to one or two days. Brevity is the soul of the minitrial because it forces concentration on what matters. Also, since business executives will be crucial participants in the minitrial, it would be impractical to expect them to devote an extended period to formal presentations. They have other work to do, too. Moreover, if the minitrial were allotted more time, there would be a real risk that it would ape the litigation process and thus be prey to all the rigidities of a trial. The strength of the process is its informality and flexibility, a strength it gains from its brevity.

Present the Best Case to Executives Empowered to Settle

These are the two most important features of the minitrial: first, that the case presented be the "best" case possible, no holds barred, no punches pulled; and second, that the case be made before representatives who have full authority to settle all aspects of the dispute with their adversaries. Without these elements the process, whatever else it might be, could not be considered a minitrial and would not be likely to succeed.

Many who first hear about the minitrial express surprise that the lawyers will in fact present the best possible case. Lawyers do not like to disclose their strategies to their adversaries, especially if, as is the case here, there is some risk that the settlement talks will fail and the case will then proceed to trial. By presenting the best case, won't your lawyer thus "give away the store"? And knowing this, won't each lawyer be tempted to reserve at least some relevant bits of information or arguments for an eventual trial?

Experience shows that in this arena the lawyers do not hold back. The primary reason is that two *business* representatives are not only present, but key participants in the process. The evidence is being shown to the business executives; the arguments are being made to the same executives. Ultimately, it is their decision that counts, not that of some judge or independent jury. To the representative of the adversary company, your lawyer will want to present a best case as a roundhouse blow in order to achieve a knockout. The lawyer's motivation here is to overwhelm the adversary, not merely the adversary's lawyer, with the cogency of the case against it. This will probably be the first time the opposing party really understands the nature of the case against it—or even that there really *is* a case to be made against it. For the lawyer to pull punches at this point would be to defeat the entire purpose of the minitrial.

Moreover, the adversary is not the only business representative in the room. The lawyer's *own client* will be there. No lawyer can afford to appear before a client looking as if he has not fully mastered the case, or seeming to be making disjointed, tangential points, when it is only the core of the case that will persuade the opposing party to yield.

Finally, for most cases that have been in discovery for any length of time, there are seldom any real secrets left. The lawyers should have little incentive, if the minitrial occurs when a case is at this stage, to hold back for fear of giving something precious away.

The minitrial is a *settlement* process. Only by soaking themselves in the facts and the law of the case, and by balancing the two, can the parties themselves, through their representatives, make an informed decision on whether to settle and for how much. Many cases fail to settle when the lawyers negotiate by themselves because neither they nor the client appreciates the realities of the situation. It is easy to fool yourself into thinking you have a stronger case than you do; it is just as easy to fool yourself into thinking the other side has a weaker case than it does. And of course the same goes for your opponent. Without a minitrial, settlement negotiations are often uninformed. Following a minitrial, the parties can assess far more accurately the probable results of a trial and take those results into account in their settlement negotiations.

Select a Neutral Advisor to Moderate and Comment If Necessary

Not every minitrial has used the services of a neutral advisor. There have been cases in which the parties met in one of the lawyers' offices and presented the evidence and hashed out the arguments. But without special circumstances, the minitrial seems to work best if the parties jointly choose a neutral adviser to moderate the proceedings when things become too heated, to keep the players to the agreed-on schedule, and to give an informed opinion on the likely outcome of the case should the business representatives fail to settle and the case go on to trial.

Professor Eric D. Green of Boston University Law School (and one of the originators of the minitrial) has identified seven reasons for preferring a third-party neutral advisor.

1. The neutral can help parties seek joint gains by devising new compromises and helping to elaborate what appears to be a single problem into an integrated negotiation with several components over which the parties can bargain. This enables the negotiators to search for and achieve a "win-win" outcome, rather than a "you lose, I win" outcome. In a minitrial, the business representatives' creativity is catalyzed by the participation of the third-party neutral.

2. The neutral can bring the parties together during the information exchange. In a minitrial, he or she often bridges the gap between the disputing parties, cuts through suspicion, and thus brings the players to the table.

3. The third party can help establish the proper procedural

ambience for negotiation before, during, and after the information exchange. The advisor helps to set the rules in the dispute, can lead the discussion, and can set an agenda. Sometimes the third party can smooth out interpersonal conflict. If necessary, the third party can prepare neutral minutes.

4. The neutral can help parties clarify values and derive reasonable prices. A third party with hands-on litigation experience can help the parties analyze their cases and advise on a settlement outcome. This is especially important when each party believes that it has a high probability of succeeding at trial. The minitrial is ideal for cases in which each side estimates that its chances of success are 75 percent or higher.

5. A neutral can deflate unreasonable claims and loosen commitments. The minitrial minimizes excessive posturing and breaks down barriers and entrenched positions. The third-party neutral allows people to see with fresh eyes.

6. The neutral can keep negotiations going when they threaten to break down. He can be an advocate for agreement. The neutral holds communications lines open and helps each side save face.

7. Finally, the neutral can articulate the rationale for agreement, thereby promoting acceptance of a solution.

These reasons will hold if the parties have done their homework and selected an appropriate neutral advisor, a person who is familiar with the industry and the types of issues that will be raised and responses that will be made. Precisely because the neutral advisor is knowledgeable, the parties will trust his or her analysis of the probable outcome of the case should it go to trial, thus giving them a far greater incentive to reach agreement on their own.

Hold Settlement Talks Immediately

Once the minitrial has concluded, the business representatives—the executives with full authority to settle—should meet immediately and privately to discuss how settlement can be reached. "Immediately" means just that: As soon as the hearings have concluded, the representatives should retire to a separate room and talk. In a few instances, representatives have waited to hear comments from the neutral advisor, or have permitted some time to go by for the advisor to seek additional evidence. But the preferred course is to talk immediately, for the simple reason that the entire case is fresh. In all likelihood a spirit of goodwill has been engendered during the course of the exchange and this can be enough to carry the representatives through what could be difficult negotiations and what certainly will be the critical moments of the entire process.

In most cases, the representatives negotiate privately— that is, without their lawyers present. If agreement is reached in principle, the lawyers will reenter the picture because they will need to put the agreement in writing. In virtually every case, the outcome of a minitrial is a contract stating the rights and obligations of the parties and explicitly providing for the termination of any pending litigation.

Provide for Confidentiality

The final common element of minitrials is confidentiality. The parties should agree in the protocol that the neutral advisor's comments and written opinion, if any, will not be offered as evidence or for any other purpose at a subsequent trial. The neutral advisor should be disqualified from acting as an advisor, expert, or in any other capacity for either of the parties at any subsequent hearings. And any documents, depositions, or statements made at the minitrial or in connection with it, including briefs submitted beforehand to the parties, should similarly be barred from use at any trial. Many agreements explicitly state that even the fact that the minitrial took place is not to be referred to in the event that the settlement discussions fail.

The protocol should not neglect the second element of

confidentiality—that the parties be spared any discussion of the proceedings by the public at large (assuming, as most do, that the parties wish to keep it secret). Again, this can be provided for easily enough in the protocol, which can bar any of the parties, the lawyers, or the neutral advisor from disclosing the existence of the agreement to conduct the minitrial and from discussing the matter before, during, or after the minitrial hearing.

Although there still remain some legal uncertainties about the extent to which every facet of the minitrial can be kept confidential, much of it certainly can be; and this assurance will provide an atmosphere in which the parties can confidently attempt to resolve the dispute quickly, cheaply, and with a minimum of rancor.

5

SEVEN ADVANTAGES OF A MINITRIAL AND WHEN TO USE IT

The minitrial has several advantages over conventional litigation. We have already mentioned many of these advantages in passing, but it is worth dwelling on them. For taken together, the minitrial's numerous benefits make clear what a remarkable tool it can be for resolving business disputes.

1. Cost Reduction

There is no statistical repository for legal expenditures, either in conventional litigation or in ADR. But we know that in the cases we have cited savings in legal expenses are at least in the hundreds of thousands of dollars. Lawyers in the NASA-TRW minitrial estimated that they saved a million dollars. In 1982, *The New York Times* reported that the cost of one minitrial was one-tenth of what the lawyers projected litigation costs would have been had the case gone to trial. But savings can even be greater than that.

Austin Industries, Inc., a large Dallas-based construction company, has used the minitrial to settle rancorous construction disputes at a saving of some 97 percent of normal litigation costs, according to J. David McClung, Austin's general counsel. Unlike most minitrials, the Austin minitrials gave a two-week breather between presentations of each case. The neutral advisor was then required to issue a report on what he thought the likely outcome would be if the case were to go to court. The parties settled on the neutral's terms within about two months. McClung says that his rule of thumb is that "anyone who litigates loses." For that reason, he has often proposed minitrials in the midst of a dispute, and "just the suggestion has several times facilitated settlements."

As we have seen, the major component of savings in minitrials lies in the drastic reduction of hours that would otherwise have been expended on pretrial discovery and on the trial itself. Especially because it involves the collection of so much peripheral information, pretrial discovery can last years. Costs associated with it include hourly billings of lawyers and staff, travel, and duplicating services. The trial itself can last for days, weeks, and in the most complex cases for months. The trial time of lawyers is always billed at top dollar, and if the court is away from the lawyers' principal offices, travel and hotel costs are likely to be considerable. Even when the trial is over costs can continue to climb precipitately, because most sizable business disputes, and many smaller ones, are appealed—a whole new undertaking that can itself take several years.

By contrast, the lengthiest minitrial will consume only several weeks of lawyers' time, virtually all of it spent on tasks that would have had to be undertaken anyway if the case had gone to trial. Moreover, because the preparation process forces the lawyers to narrow the issues and sharpen the focus of the dispute, it may actually save money in the event that the minitrial proves unsuccessful, for the lawyers will be able to prepare more efficiently for trial.

That the preparation process focuses the case can be clearly seen from the American Can Company–Wisconsin Electric Power Company minitrial. American Can sued Wisconsin Electric for $41 million for breach of contract over the use of industrial waste it was selling to Wisconsin Electric as boiler fuel. Wisconsin Electric countersued for $20 million, claiming that its costs in burning the wastes were $20 million more than it was contractually obligated to pay. The technical issues were numerous and intricate. It was estimated that the trial would take at least seventy-five days in court. Seven months into the discovery, the parties decided to attempt to settle through a minitrial, and signed on as their neutral advisor former Federal District Judge Harold R. Tyler, Jr., senior partner of the New York law firm of Patterson Belknap Webb & Tyler.

Before the three-day hearing, the lawyers supplied Judge Tyler and the business representatives with several hundred exhibits and brief summaries (fewer than thirty pages for each side) of the parties' arguments and positions. As Robert H. Gorske, vice-president and general counsel of Wisconsin Electric, later stated, the abbreviated hearing forced the parties to focus in a way that rarely happens in court:

> Although the basic case and the counterclaim were both extremely complex, the neutral advisor and his fellow panel members had by the end of the oral argument period on the third day a complete grasp of what the significant points of the two sides were. Further, all those present had better understandings of the arguments of each side and how convincing they were. This kind of result is extremely difficult (but not impossible) to achieve in the usual procedure in which the trial counsel reports to his client management about such matters.

Over the next several days, the parties met alone and with Judge Tyler, who candidly evaluated the various arguments and said what he thought the chances of ultimate success in court would be. In three months, the case was settled through private negotiations between the company representatives, eliminating the seventy-five trial days and many months of protracted discovery.

The only costs in these proceedings that would not be borne at trial are the immediate costs of the information exchange and the neutral advisor. Since the information exchange part of the minitrial lasts two or three days, the time involved is minuscule. The neutral advisor is paid either an hourly fee (which could be as high as $250 or $300 or more for top-flight professionals), or a negotiated flat fee, which might go as high as several thousand dollars. Against the total cost of the case this fee is relatively inexpensive, and it is usually divided equally among the parties. Moreover, in many trials expert witnesses will command similar fees (both for testifying at trial and for helping the parties prepare for trial), and these fees are often avoided altogether if the minitrial is successful.

So as a most liberal guess, the minitrial of a complex business dispute may result in a nonrecoverable cost to each company of between $10,000 and $20,000. The disputants will not be able to recoup this money if the minitrial fails and they eventually wind up in court. But against the costs that will be incurred without ADR, this is a tiny expense, well worth the risk.

2. Creative Problem-Solving

The minitrial greatly enhances the opportunity for a "win-win" resolution of the dispute that is dividing the parties. In courtroom litigation, the judge is bound to make a ruling on the law that usually will give an "all or nothing" verdict to one side. There is precious little room for compromise, because the judicial forum (and for that matter, arbitration) does not operate as a negotiator, but as an adjudicator of legal rights: Either the plaintiff has a legal right to what it asks, or it does not. Moreover, what is relevant in the courtroom are only those facts and circumstances directly relating to the case at issue. In a breach of contract case, for example, judge and jury will consider whether there was a legally binding contract, whether it was breached, and what damages were suffered. But they will not be interested in whether the plaintiff and defendant are parties to other, unrelated contracts. Why should they be interested? The short answer is that when two parties have ongoing relations, there is almost always a way of bringing other aspects of the relationship into the picture to effect a compromise—if the parties try to do so outside the courtroom.

The most dramatic example of this extrajudicial compromise is the Texaco-Borden minitrial. In May 1980, the Borden Company filed a $200 million antitrust suit against Texaco, Inc., in connection with a natural gas contract in Louisiana. Both sides were initially confident of their claims and defenses, and so the lawyers dug in. Texaco lawyers, for example, expended many thousands of billable hours, and the company produced some 300,000 documents during discovery. So complex was the case that the federal district judge scheduled a preliminary jury trial two and a half years later merely to "interpret the contract" in the hope of limiting discovery.

A few weeks before the November 1982 trial date, Borden counsel H. Blair White of the Chicago law firm of Sidley & Austin discussed with Texaco general counsel William Weitzel, Jr., the possibility of a minitrial. They established simple ground rules. The parties would meet on neutral ground—in a private room in New York's Union League Club—and argue the case to executive vice-presidents of each company (James W. Kinnear of Texaco and Robert Gutheil of Borden). The lawyers would each have an hour to present their cases, plus time for rebuttal, though, as White put it, "no one was holding a stopwatch." Each company was also permitted to have advisors other than lawyers. Texaco had present a Louisiana operations manager, and Borden had high-level operations and financial experts.

The hearing went smoothly, but the private discussions over dinner between Kinnear and Gutheil did not. Gutheil wound up pressing for even more money than White had demanded, and Texaco's Kinnear was so convinced of his position that he "was reluctant to assign even nuisance value to Borden's claim." In fact, Kinnear contemplated pressing counterclaims against Borden.

At this point the outcome looked dim, but the parties did not break off negotiations. They agreed to talk by telephone in a few days, and these conversations led to still others. Their persistence paid off: Within a few weeks the dispute was resolved in a manner never anticipated in the litigation. Indeed, it was settled in a manner that would never have been possible had the dispute been taken to court.

The companies wound up renegotiating a gas supply contract that had not even been at issue in the original case. They also created a new arrangement for transporting Texaco gas to Borden at prices favorable to Borden. This settlement resulted in a "nine-digit benefit" to Borden that was expected to give Texaco "positive earnings in cash flow," according to Texaco associate general counsel Charles F. Kazlauskas, Jr. The resulting contracts enabled both Borden and Texaco to claim victory. "That is truly a win-win situation, which we never expected," Kazlauskas has said. He noted that the parties learned five basic lessons from the experience:

1. The litigation pending in the background provided a strong incentive for settlement.

2. The mutually beneficial settlement could never have been achieved in court, however, because courts lack the power and expertise to fashion a complex remedy involving far more than the simple payment of money. Lawyers acting alone probably would not have been able to devise such a settlement. "The magic was the creativity of two extremely knowledgeable businessmen who recognized each others' strengths and weaknesses. By repositioning these business realities, they were able to make both sides winners."

3. Nevertheless, the results could not have been produced without the lawyers. Without their "persuasive presentations," the executives would never have fully recognized the hazards of litigation, such as the ambiguities of documents and other evidence.

4. The settlement dramatically changed the companies' working environments. What had been a tense adversary

environment was transformed into an attitude of cooperation.

5. The settlement was achieved without the anticipated immense expenditure of money and time, without the business disruption that would have ensued had the trial gone forward (and without the almost inevitable appeals and potential retrials). Concluded Kazlauskas: "I think the minitrial alternative should always be considered when a potentially complex business dispute arises, especially in inter-firm disputes between Fortune 500 corporations."

By taking their differences to a minitrial, both companies were able to bring into the picture their other contracts, and to work out a deal that made economic sense to both. They were able to expand their opportunities by considering their entire business relationship. This was a business solution that could never have been contemplated by their lawyers, at least their outside lawyers. No court, no jury, no litigation can achieve what they achieved.

3. Preservation of Continuing Relationships

Minitrials have invariably preserved important business relationships, relationships that are typically lost in the acrimony of litigation. This preservation has often been cited as the most important result of successful minitrials. In the Control Data Corporation construction minitrial of 1982, architects, contractors, and builders would have lost a lucrative source of future work had they been unable to resolve amicably the problem of a leaking glass wall. Because they did resolve it, Control Data was amenable to employing them in the future as it had in the past.

It began as something more than Control Data's contractors had bargained for: They built the company's corporate headquarters in Minneapolis with a fourteen-story glass wall that leaked whenever it rained. Rather than rushing to sue, Control Data tried to talk the various participants in the fiasco into repairing the flaw. But two large contractors, a construction company, the glass manufacturer, and a host of subcontractors declined to provide any remedy. Finding no alternative, Control Data sued all of them for the several million dollars it would take to make the repairs.

The trouble was that everyone pointed a finger at everyone else, and several fingers pointed back at Control Data, which itself does considerable construction work around the world. At an early meeting with lawyers for several of the parties, Control Data's then general counsel Lawrence Perlman suggested using some form of minitrial. Rather than start up what promised to be a round of massive discovery, the principal parties—Control Data, the architects, and the builders—agreed to try the process to apportion liability among themselves; they avoided involving the subcontractors at that stage.

Each of the three groups appointed a senior manager with full authority to settle the case. Each side had seventy-five minutes to present its case and to question the others. Initially, the parties' lawyers specified that neutral outside engineers, architects, and a lawyer would sit with the managers. But, striving for simplicity, the managers eliminated these neutrals from the ground rules.

Following the five-hour presentation, the managers met in Perlman's office at headquarters and talked. After about ninety minutes, a settlement emerged. It involved the payment to Control Data of several million dollars and an arrangement that would permit the contractor and the architect to replace the outside of the building piece by piece, at their expense, over a three-year period. The solution was "eminently fair and practical," said Perlman, who noted that it was a more flexible arrangement than a court would have been able to construct. Following this agreement, the contractor and the architect negotiated for about three months to secure contributions from the subcontractors.

The net result of the process, Perlman concluded, was to preserve the business relationships. "We will use these contractors and these architects again," he said at the time of the settlement. "I can guarantee you as the person who makes those decisions that if we had gone to court with them, further business relationships would have been very difficult to maintain."

4. Choice of Neutral Advisor

In federal courts and many state courts, judges are selected to preside over a particular case through a random drawing. The judge's experience and knowledge do not enter into the selection. A judge with no patent or antitrust experience may find himself presiding over a complex patent-antitrust case as easily as a judge with much prior experience. The minitrial (and other private processes, too) permit the parties to choose their own neutral advisor, one who is known to be well equipped to deal with the technical, legal, scientific, and other esoteric issues in the case. In a recent minitrial involving a major construction company and utility, the use of a respected engineer as neutral advisor gave credibility to the decision for the power utility, which might otherwise have balked at settling.

5. A Tailor-Made Process

The minitrial enables the parties to design their own process rules. This is a decided advantage over litigation, whose formal rules of procedure and evidence can distort issues and lead the litigants into a blind alley. A set of rules tailored to the type of case and the personalities of the players can make the proceeding efficient, limit the time that needs to be spent at the hearing, and relieve the frustration that comes from being unable to put forward a coherent case all at one time.

6. Maintenance of Confidentiality

No one wants to publicize an alleged mistake or a dispute with an important business partner. But formal litigation, at least if it reaches the courtroom, takes place in the proverbial goldfish bowl. The courtroom is open to the public, which for important business cases means an inquiring press; in a big enough case, the whole world will know the intimate facts. Nor is disclosure of sensitive business facts limited to what is spoken in the courtroom itself; most documents produced in the case and introduced in court are available for outside inspection also.

Not so in the minitrial. As we have seen, the parties can operate under tight secrecy rules they draw up themselves. Nothing need be disclosed before, during, or after the successful minitrial. The proceeding itself is held in secrecy: No outsider need be invited; indeed, no outsider even need know that it is taking place. Documents remain the property of the parties, who retain them when the hearing is over. The neutral advisor is pledged to say nothing about what he hears (and sometimes even to refrain from saying that he served as a neutral advisor), and he is barred from serving either party as an expert witness or in any other capacity in connection with the particular case.

This was the situation when two major oil companies used a minitrial to settle a $28 million claim for cost overruns on the construction of a supertanker. One of the oil companies was buying a pair of Alaska oil trade tankers; the other company owned the shipyard that was late in making them. Although the parties were barely on speaking terms, they hesitated to go through a projected five years of litigation, and they especially feared the attendant publicity. So they presented their cases in six hours before a three-member panel: the president of the shipyard, the general counsel of the shipyard's parent company, and a vice-president of the buyer. The settlement came about two weeks after the six-hour hearing, and the customer got about half of what it demanded. The parties say they were impressed with the process, but they still won't disclose their identities—a luxury they would not have been permitted had they wound up in court.

7. Dramatic Time Savings

A business executive speaking to the annual conference of the judges of the Ninth Circuit Federal Court of Appeals recently described justice as the right of a corporation to have its decade in court. In a fast-moving marketplace, with product lives of twelve and eighteen months and with increasing foreign competition, dispute resolution measured in weeks and months is far superior to litigation measured in years. The biggest cost of litigation increasingly cited by business is lost business opportunities, lost because of the shadow of litigation that makes executives hesitant to act until it is settled.

Compared to formal litigation, the time of preparing for the minitrial is slight indeed. Most corporate lawsuits require months of preparation at a minimum, and years in complicated cases. Protracted litigation can absorb an outsized allocation of management's time just in peripheral discovery. A minitrial can be constructed and completed in a matter of a few months; the hearing itself will last two days, rather than weeks or months. In a minitrial, the time required of key managers, even though they play the dominant role, is quite limited.

In the early 1980s, many top corporate lawyers met periodically to talk about alternative dispute resolution, and the chief topic of conversation was the minitrial. They worried then as they do today: Will their suggestion to the CEO and top management that the company try to resolve a dispute through ADR be greeted with skepticism? Will they be viewed as soft-headed and weak?

Thus in 1981 John Stichnoth, general counsel of Union

Carbide Corporation and one of the earliest proponents of ADR, counseled many of his brethren about jumping too fast, because the "wrong case" could ruin ADR's chances within a particular company if the lawyers resorted to it under adverse circumstances and found it wanting. Managers, he said, may permit themselves to be talked into an experiment, but they will not be likely to repeat a novelty if it goes wrong the first time.

Minitrials are no longer a sport, no longer an aberration. To the contrary, among those who have used the minitrial to settle disputes are some of America's largest and best-known corporations—Allied Corporation, Amoco, Austin Industries, Continental Can, Control Data Corporation, Gillette Company, Shell Oil Company, Union Carbide Corporation, and Wisconsin Electric Power Company. Moreover, the types of disputes settled through the minitrial process are varied; they include contracts, antitrust, product liability, insurance claims, construction, trade secrets, and employee disputes. The minitrial has proved its worth not simply as a theoretical technique, but as a practical device of widespread utility.

6

DETERRENTS
TO THE MINITRIAL

Despite the range of legal disputes to which the minitrial has
been applied, it is not a panacea. It cannot be used as a
substitute for every lawsuit. In this chapter, we note circumstances under which the minitrial might not be an appropriate
means of resolving legal disputes. Even so, because the minitrial
is flexible and adaptable, we report some cases and suggest
some reasons for thinking that the minitrial might have broader
uses than has been supposed.

Counsel's Unfamiliarity

Perhaps the single biggest deterrent to the use of the minitrial
is the lawyer's lack of familiarity with it. Although there has
been considerable comment on the minitrial within legal
circles in the 1980s, only a relatively small percentage of the
practicing bar has any knowledge of the minitrial and its
success record. (In Further Reading, we have listed a few
works to which your lawyer can refer for further information.)

The lawyer's unfamiliarity is not inevitably a deterrent,
however, as the Gillette trade secrets minitrial demonstrates.
A Gillette employee quit his job to join another company,
allegedly taking with him trade secrets involving writing in-
struments that Gillette manufactured. The employee joined a
competing manufacturer, which quickly brought a similar
product to market. Gillette sued, claiming theft of trade secrets
and patent infringement.

From the very outset, Joseph E. Mullaney, Gillette senior
vice-president and general counsel, sought a way to short-

48

circuit the litigation. A telephone call from Gillette's divisional vice-president to the competitor's president (who had also once worked for Gillette) failed to lead to a settlement. The competitor was prepared to file an antitrust countersuit.

When Mullaney suggested a minitrial, his counterpart was quick to agree. The only dissenter was Gillette's outside lawyer, who peppered Mullaney with objections; the minitrial could not possibly work, he said. Eventually, the outside lawyer presented Mullaney with a lengthy memorandum denouncing the minitrial protocol. "The memo was a classic statement of the traditional position that only litigation would work," Mullaney recalled. He firmly disagreed and "put our outside counsel on the shelf. He didn't trust the opposing lawyers; I did. So we went forward."

The protocol provided for limited document discovery and a tight timetable for examining the parties. The two companies hoped to finish the case in four months, but the schedule slipped a bit and it took six. In the end, after listening to the lawyers' presentations, Gillette's divisional vice-president and the competitor's president met for a morning with the lawyers and then, over lunch, reached substantial agreement. The signed agreement provided for "some dollars to change hands," for the defendant to take a license on Gillette's patent, and for Gillette to take an option on any patents that the defendant might obtain. The minitrial thus avoided virtually all the expenses of litigation and settled the case in perhaps a sixth of the time that it might have taken in court.

The clear loser, says Mullaney, was Gillette's outside lawyer. In opposing the minitrial idea, "he argued that the courtroom is the only crucible for getting at the truth." As Mullaney notes, "that's rather farfetched these days."

Tactical Use of Litigation

When one of the parties is using litigation as a tactic to achieve some other end than simply winning a judgment (for instance, to gain publicity for a particular cause), the mutual consent necessary to initiate a minitrial will be lacking. Even so, the parties in many such lawsuits are also seeking a reasonable outcome, and the smart litigator might consider the possibility of gaining as much publicity value by securing an appropriate settlement through a minitrial as through a bitter court fight.

Litigation to Defer Liability

It is no secret that defendants drag out many lawsuits in order to defer payment for damages they caused. Under the rules in most jurisdictions, no interest needs to be paid on many damage awards until the moment the judgment is handed down. (By contrast, proof of a claim that the defendant failed to make a required contractual payment will result in an award for the amount owed plus interest dating from the time the original amount was due.) In many jurisdictions, court-ordered interest is considerably lower than real interest rates. So on both grounds, it will often pay a defendant to defer a finding of liability and damages as long as possible. In such a case, the defendant is unlikely to agree to resolve the dispute by minitrial. With interest rates now declining from their historic highs in the early 1980s, however, this should become a less persuasive reason for dragging out the lawsuit.

Lack of Trust

The minitrial requires some minimum level of trust among the professionals (lawyers and executives). If mutual feelings have reached too low an ebb, mutual suspicions will be too serious to allow one side to agree to the other's suggestion that something other than conventional litigation be used. This is not necessarily because the refusing party will doubt the efficacy of ADR: He or she may simply be unable to swallow a suggestion by an adversary that they engage in a cooperative venture. One possible way to break down the barriers of mutual suspicion is to have a neutral intermediary, acceptable to the adversary, explore the possibility of structuring settlement talks (see Chapter 9).

Credibility of Witnesses

The conventional wisdom has it that when a case revolves around the credibility of key witnesses, it will be hard to resolve through a minitrial. Certain authors suggest that credibility issues are inherently incapable of being resolved in an objective fashion; hence, the executives will be obliged to sort out the facts (or fantasies) after the hearing is over. How to deal with the facts as they exist is something with which experienced negotiators can cope. How to determine the facts is not. It is always possible, of course, to show that a witness is flat-out lying, but rarely is direct evidence available. In most issues where credibility is key, the witnesses may seem not to be deliberately lying, but rather to be stating their different (and sincerely felt) versions of the truth. In a minitrial, this presents too sticky a situation for the executives to attempt to resolve.

That is the argument, but we believe more evidence is in order before such a conclusion can be justified. Executives at this level—savvy business managers—are far more sophisticated than the average jury called upon to determine who is lying in a case and who is not. In these disputes the executives are probably the best judges of who is lying, not the worst. Indeed, a party that knows its own witness is likely to appear incredible is advised to think long and hard before presenting that witness at a minitrial.

"Pure" Legal Questions as Sole Issues

At the other extreme are cases in which the only live issues are legal ones—for example, whether a certain marketing arrangement violates the Sherman Act. The conventional wisdom holds that such cases are better left to the so-called summary judgment procedures of the courts, in which judges need not submit the case to a jury for findings, but simply hear and make rulings on the law. But it is not necessarily true that these "pure law" cases can never successfully be heard in a minitrial procedure. The opinion of a neutral advisor who is a retired judge or an expert in the particular field of law may tell the parties much about whether it makes sense to continue the case or to reach a compromise based on the advisor's opinion. In our judgment, the minitrial is still too new to write off the possibility of using it in cases involving only questions of law.

In 1984, when Honeywell and Telecredit engaged in a dispute about the meaning of a contract provision involving payment of a $100,000 license fee, the facts were undisputed. The dispute turned on whether a particular clause in the contract required Honeywell to make one payment or two before exercising an option to cancel the deal. The amount in dispute was too small to take to court, so the parties designated an arbitrator to make a "legal" ruling on the meaning of the contract clause. The parties resorted to an arbitrator because they wished the outcome to be binding; had they not, they could as easily have had their managers listen to the debate in a minitrial format.

However, it certainly is true that there will be no consent to a minitrial if one side is litigating because it *wants* a court ruling in order to establish a new rule of law. In certain types of cases, the plaintiff may be seeking a legal ruling or the reaffirmation of a policy. For example, a public interest plaintiff may be seeking a court ruling on the meaning of an environmental statute, or the government may be seeking to vindicate its policy of filing certain kinds of lawsuits. When these elements are present, the plaintiff may feel that its interests are not served by a minitrial.

Missing Executives

Some cases may not lend themselves to the presence of executives. In the typical product liability case, for example, an insurance company executive and manufacturing company executive can attend the hearing, but there is no executive on the plaintiff's side. There is only the plaintiff or the plaintiff's lawyer. This can be a barrier to successful resolution. In some cases, however, this barrier can be surmounted, as a Union Carbide case shows.

In late 1977 and early 1978, eighteen factory workers claimed that an industrial chemical manufactured by Union Carbide had made them ill on the job. Union Carbide took the product off the market. The workers filed typical product liability suits to recover money damages for their injuries. Union Carbide asserted a "state-of-the-art" defense; it had, it said, followed the current state of chemical knowledge, which gave no warning of the product's potential toxic effect. The workers' damages were relatively modest; they all recovered from their illnesses and missed no days of work. Their claim was largely for discomfort.

The lawyers began to consider the minitrial at a very early stage of the litigation. Indeed, none of the plaintiffs had undergone depositions or been given physical examinations. Had the cases proceeded along the usual route, they would have taken another five years, according to Robert A. Butler, Union Carbide's chief litigator.

The parties agreed on a minitrial protocol. Butler, together with a key Union Carbide executive and a member of the outside law firm representing the company, met with Ed Swartz, the plaintiff's counsel, in Swartz's Boston law office (a historical site: it was once the kitchen in the house where John Hancock lived). The minitrial lasted a full day. Although they dispensed with a neutral advisor, the process was orderly. No one shouted; each had respect for the others. Swartz presented evidence for each plaintiff, and Butler and his co-counsel would caucus, discuss the evidence, and then return to discuss the claims some more. Gradually, each side began to give—the easiest cases first, and finally the hardest.

Butler distinguishes what happened in John Hancock's kitchen from the ordinary informal settlement discussion, and he insists that the minitrial process was an important factor in producing the settlement. "The minitrial format requires the key people to be present, which doesn't happen often at informal discussions. Also, you know that you won't get the chance to do this again, so you go for your best case. And it does make a difference before you talk numbers to tell what your case is and hear directly what their case is."

To what extent a minitrial would work in a more complex product liability case, or one involving larger damage claims, remains unknown.

Large or Crippling Judgments

In some cases, plaintiffs seek what to the defendant amounts to large or even crippling judgments. When the plaintiff, or the plaintiff's lawyer, genuinely expects or at least hopes for a giant verdict, or one that would cripple the defendant, a minitrial may not work. It is argued that the reason the Union Carbide product liability minitrial worked was that the plaintiffs ultimately recovered from their injuries and their damages were relatively minor compared to those involved in many product liability claims.

This criterion is at best only a very general one, and specific circumstances may dictate the prudence of trying a minitrial anyway. The size of damages is relative to the size of the company, its assets, revenues, business prospects, and the risk that others will bring similar claims. Moreover, the mere demand for large damages does not prove a strong belief by the plaintiff in the likelihood of recovering them, and the minitrial setting may provide both sides an opportunity to see that the issues and claims can be negotiated.

Desire for a Jury

Some plaintiffs will want their cases heard by a jury in the first instance, because they suppose that the particular facts (such as the nature of the injury in a personal injury case) may make their claim especially compelling to a jury. Even here it is possible to convince a plaintiff's lawyer otherwise— if, for example, he is seeking a way to avoid having to bankroll a suit against a large company with financial staying power.

Unequal Bargaining Power

Some people doubt that a minitrial will work when a very large company is pitted against a small one. But the very first minitrial consisted of just such parties—giant TRW and relatively tiny Telecredit. Whether or not a minitrial will work depends on the willingness of both sides to settle, given a reasonable way to proceed.

Exceptional cases may resist the solutions offered by the minitrial, but the field remains wide open for reasonable experimentation. Whenever the dispute involves parties who have or desire to have a continuing relationship (employee and employer, buyer and seller, joint venturers, licensor and licensee), the minitrial will ordinarily be an ideal vehicle. We do not mean to say that the minitrial under these circumstances will always work; there are no guarantees. But few are willing to discard relationships they have put considerable time and money into building. The cost of finding new partners (employees, customers, suppliers) can be high; it is obviously preferable to continue doing business with those you know, if your dispute can be reasonably and amicably resolved. The possibility of reaching a mutually advantageous solution is certainly worth the initial exploration and minimal outlay of dollars and time required for a minitrial. More cannot be said of any dispute resolution process.

7

MEDIATION:
THE SLEEPING GIANT OF
BUSINESS DISPUTE
RESOLUTION

When we think of the mediator, we tend to picture bleary-eyed negotiators, cold coffee in their cups, slumped around a conference table as the sun rises. Having reached an impasse, late in their negotiations, the parties have called in a third-party intermediary, the mediator, in a last-ditch effort to get the picketers back to work, or stand the armies down from general alert. In dusk-to-dawn discussions, the mediator tries to lead the parties toward agreement.

An obvious example that springs to mind is international mediation—for example, the Camp David talks that produced the Egyptian-Israeli peace treaty in 1979 succeeded because a third-party mediator, President Carter, managed to bring the disputants together and show them that their common interests outweighed their mutual antagonisms. And an Algerian statesman acting as mediator played a crucial role in forging the agreement that freed the American hostages from Teheran.

This is not an unfair picture, for frequently the mediator is summoned to help end a crisis—or avert an even larger one. But it is not a complete picture. Irving S. Shapiro, retired chairman of Du Pont, put his finger on quite a different role for the mediator, a role so far not widely employed—as an aid to resolution at a very *early* stage of a business dispute. Mediation is the sleeping giant of business dispute resolution because it is potentially the most powerful means of bringing the parties to terms.

Unlike the arbitrator (Chapter 8) or the judge, the mediator has no authority to make a binding decision. For that matter, the mediator has no authority to make any sort of determination. The mediator's role is purely facilitative: He helps bring the parties together by listening, counseling, guiding, suggesting, and persuading the parties to come to terms. As a neutral, the mediator is an agent for neither of the parties, a member of neither of the negotiating teams. He is an adjunct to negotiations that the parties might carry on directly.

In the typical negotiation (a process we explore in Chapter 9), the parties must guess at each other's strategy and bottom line. The personalities of the negotiators and the circumstances of the dispute may give incentives to fudge or lie, to dig in one's heels and stubbornly refuse to compromise, to misinterpret what the other party is saying. Or the parties may be so overcome by anger and mutual hostility that they cannot sit down to talk over their differences. These problems can be overcome with the right mediator.

Mediation succeeds by blending two key factors in any negotiation: communication and trust. The mediator must be a person whom the parties trust sufficiently to communicate confidentially their real positions in the dispute. A mediator should have the respect of each party, so that each will entrust to the mediator a statement of what that party "really wants." This is the crux of the process. A person who knows the facts, and who also has intimate details of both positions, will be able to gauge the difference that lies between them in a way that negotiators who know only their own side never can. With this knowledge, the mediator will be able to forge options that the parties themselves might never have conceived.

When the parties do agree, it is their *own* agreement. No one forced them to it. No coercion is ever used, because the mediator has no power to impose a settlement. And since the agreement is one the parties mutually arrive at, they tend to accept it and live by it with far less resentment than they would a court decree.

To take a simple example, suppose the parties are trying to settle a dispute arising out of an alleged breach of contract. One party denies the breach; the other vehemently asserts it and asks for $200,000 damages. Suppose the defendant in fact admits privately that the plaintiff's claim has considerable merit, but that he will not pay more than $125,000. Suppose that the plaintiff admits to uncertainty about his ability to prove the claim and says that he overstated the damages in order to collect in the neighborhood of $150,000. In simple head-to-head negotiations, neither party is likely to budge because each thinks itself far apart from the other. But the mediator should be able to suggest to each party privately a compromise position that will work.

Since mediation is a process as unstructured and informal as direct negotiation, it has no required ground rules. Mediators may work in a variety of ways, suiting their mediating styles to the personalities and needs of the parties in each instance. Nevertheless, there is a core responsibility: to respect the confidentiality of disclosures made by each party. If the mediator deems it strategically necessary that one side learn something of the other's case, he or she may ask permission to disclose all or part of what has been revealed. But the mediator must keep secret what has been confided as a secret.

Trained mediators understand that part of their role is to defuse the hostilities that have built up during the prior course of dealings between the parties. As neutral third-party intermediaries, mediators can deflect the raw emotion that so often prevents the parties from negotiating directly.

In seeking to facilitate agreement, mediators may propose steps to be taken, partial solutions, or a comprehensive deal. Good mediators will do so by respecting the parties' wishes and by helping them negotiate their own solution. They will rarely take over the negotiations on their own. Many commentators have compared the mediator to a catalyst, one who prompts action by others through identification of issues, clarification of facts, reason, and persuasion. In doing so, mediators will help educate each party (at least those with a continuing relationship) not merely for the resolution of the present dispute, but for the resolution and even prevention of future disputes.

Any private civil case may go to mediation; no law restricts its use or governs its availability. The parties simply need agree, either in advance of a dispute or during one, to call in a mediator to help them iron out their differences.

Not every case, though, is necessarily ripe for mediation. Here are some circumstances in which mediation is most useful:

1. *Emotionalism.* The mediator will help discharge the buildup of tension and get the parties to work together. The mediator can help restore a rational dialogue, thus permitting the parties to come to terms unburdened by unnecessary side issues. When the attempt to settle a dispute is bogged down in hostility and mutual suspicion, the mediator can open up the channels of discussion.

2. *Impasse.* When the parties reach an impasse, a mediator can often find ways around it. The mediator can bring a fresh perspective and can point to potential compromises that the parties, suffering from incomplete knowledge of both sides of the case, did not think possible. Moreover, the mediator can often do this in a way foreclosed to either side. Many times a disputant will see a possible approach to resolution but will refrain from raising it because he will fear that the other side will view him as weak or will interpret the suggestion as a willingness to compromise a previously firm position. When the suggestion comes from the mediator, both sides can discuss it without being afraid that they have given anything away.

3. *Complexity.* When the issues are complex, a mediator can help untangle them and give perspective to the whole

range of questions facing the parties. A good mediator can see both the forest and the trees.

4. *No obvious right answer.* A corollary of the problem of complexity is that many disputes have no obvious right answer. If the parties are open to compromise, the mediator can help them locate it by working actively to construct a solution.

A famous example in the literature has a dowager willing an extensive painting collection to two museums. The only instructions are that each museum is to get an "equal" share of the collection. Obviously, it is not sufficient simply to let each museum take an equal *number* of canvases at random, for any given division may result in a widely divergent worth to each and an equally divergent utility. (A museum with many Picassos might prefer a single Rembrandt to two or three more Picassos.) Although some answers to the dilemma are better than others, there is no obvious right or wrong solution to the task of dividing the paintings equally. A mediator can help the museums formulate and focus their own interests in order to locate the common ground for dividing the bequest.

5. *Multiple parties.* A mediator can be exceedingly helpful in resolving a dispute involving multiple parties. This is a role some judges now play in court when a tangled case involves several plaintiffs or defendants. If the issues are complex enough and the parties numerous enough, a mediator might be the *only* person who can bring about a settlement because he or she can manage the process when no one else is in charge. We will shortly see one example of multiparty mediation.

6. *Urgency.* Sometimes both disputants urgently need their quarrel settled—for instance, with winter approaching, construction may be halted pending the resolution of a dispute between builder and architect. A mediator can be of immense value in this situation, because he or she can gauge the

willingness of the parties to talk, and can schedule meetings and put forth an agenda calculated to wring a maximally beneficial agreement from all concerned.

Mediation has become quite popular in some areas. It has long thrived in the field of labor relations. Both federal and state laws specify that some types of labor disputes must be mediated. In federal labor disputes, the Federal Mediation and Conciliation Service exists to do just that.

Beyond labor disputes, mediation services have developed during the past five years or more for a variety of more or less personal disputes. Around the country, some 400 private and governmental agencies provide mediation services. Thus, a whole new class of mediators has developed to mediate disputes involving family affairs—primarily those concerning divorce and child custody. Probably no city today is without one or more mediation plans or companies, some for profit, offering these services.

In many court systems, petty crimes, such as breach of the peace, and small related civil disputes are referred by consent of the parties to mediators who have undertaken by contract with the courts to resolve the disputes (or, in the case of crimes, to obtain the pledge of the defendants not to repeat their actions). Several cities have so-called Neighborhood Justice Centers, which act as adjuncts of the court to perform the same functions. And a few courts are beginning to experiment with mediation as a first-line alternative to adjudication (for a brief description of one such program, see Chapter 13).

Finally, some large-scale (and highly publicized) disputes have been resolved through mediation. Chicago hired a mediator to put an end to its decade-long suit over the racial segregation of its schools. Many environmental disputes, unresolved for years or even decades, have finally been settled through the active involvement of mediators.

One important example was the mediation of the Storm King Mountain dispute between Consolidated Edison, the New York electric utility company, and numerous environmental groups. Con Edison proposed to build a pumped-storage plant at Storm King Mountain on the Hudson River. To cool the plant's condensers, the plant would need to draw in from the river some 4 million gallons of water a minute. Environmentalists charged that 33 to 40 percent of the Hudson's striped bass would be killed if the plant were built, with deleterious effects on the river as a whole. The Environmental Protection Agency demanded that Con Edison install closed-cycle cooling towers. Lawsuits were filed in 1965, and they were still going fifteen years later. Then, in April 1979, the parties called in Russell Train, former EPA administrator, and asked him to serve as a mediator. During the next fourteen months, the parties met with Train about twenty times. As mediator, he later wrote: "My role was generally limited to chairing the meetings, seeing to it that another meeting was always scheduled and that the parties had certain tasks to perform before the next meeting." Occasionally he called for progress reports between meetings, and when necessary he intervened with the government to break a logjam that threatened the talks. Eventually the parties—including, significantly, EPA, which was the last holdout—made a deal; Train announced the so-called Hudson River Peace Treaty in December 1980, achieving in fourteen months what litigation had failed to yield in more than fifteen years.

Mediation is beginning to find uses too in areas once thought to be the exclusive province of the courts—for instance, personal injury litigation. Perhaps the most dramatic recent example is the effort, still underway, to forge consensus among the various interests in the largest class of disputes in American history, measured either by dollar volume or number of litigants—the asbestos lawsuits. Stemming from diseases allegedly caused by exposure to asbestos going back four decades or more, some 20,000 lawsuits have been filed to date against dozens of producers and insurers. More than $38 billion in potential awards to plaintiffs is at stake (and defense costs will total, it has been estimated, some $30 billion).

In 1982, Harry H. Wellington, then dean of the Yale Law School and a member of the Center for Public Resources Judicial Panel (see Chapter 10), convened a group of asbestos producers, insurers, and plaintiffs' counsel to engage in a two-year mediation to ascertain how the unacceptably high legal costs in these cases could be reduced. (One study has shown that $2.71 was being spent to get $1 into the hands of claimants.)

Known to the group as the "facilitator" or "moderator," Wellington asked each set of participants at the outset to educate himself and two other neutrals about the asbestos litigation from their own perspective. Because there were numerous conflicts and disagreements even within each industry, as well as between them, it was essential that the groups begin to communicate.

The producers were sharply split. The Manville Corporation was seeking a solution through corporate reorganization in bankruptcy court; the other producers seem committed to alternative methods for resolving their difficulties. Accentuating the rift among the producers was their conflicting position on how to calculate their share of the liability. Each producer's attitude toward settlement was also influenced by the amount of insurance purchased over the years and the amount of coverage that insurance afforded. Unlike the insurers (substantial insurance money is available for indemnification and defense), "the producers had nothing in common except asbestos litigation," Dean Wellington later remarked. And precisely because they did not do business with each other, the ability of the producers to communicate among themselves was undermined.

The insurers too had conflicts. One reason Dean Wellington labeled "structural": There were different types of insurers and insurance coverage. The coverage afforded by primary insurers and their duty to defend lawsuits could conflict with the interests and obligations of the excess-coverage insurers. Another reason was that insurers took different positions concerning the period of time for which each was responsible to pay out. Some said that insurance was due an injured person from the time the disease first became manifest; others said payment was due from the time of first exposure.

The relationship between the insurers and the producers was even worse. The most divisive issue was the extent of coverage. So contentious was this issue that the insurers and the producers "could barely look at each other, let alone talk to each other." It became clear to Dean Wellington that the producers and insurers would have to meet out of earshot of the plaintiff's representatives if they were to resolve these profound disagreements. Because the two groups would "frequently reach an impasse in ways that made it extremely difficult for them to reconvene," Wellington believes that "the most significant contribution made by the neutrals was keeping the parties talking." Even so, at this stage of the discussions, the parties made little progress because they "did not even trust each other enough to negotiate."

Wellington kept them talking. One of his most effective techniques was to provide the insurers with a "disinterested view of where the law was going with respect to coverage." From this analysis, the insurers came to realize that it was quite probable they would have to settle on terms they had previously considered unpalatable. Communication between insurers and neutrals was enhanced because companies within the insurance industry do business together and were accustomed to "discussing disagreements before people who were not in the industry."

The mediation finally began to progress when the negotiation teams were made smaller, so that as the parties came to know each other, they learned to trust each other. Through this trust, and through the course of the year-long discussions, they came to realize that the common interest of all in finding some resolution to the tangled web of asbestos cases was paramount over individual interests.

The outcome, Wellington asserts, "was primarily influenced by the background law, and the limits of what could be negotiated were constantly narrowed by those legal principles." The outcome was made possible also by the "extraordinary capability of the negotiators," some lawyers, some business executives.

What the mediation produced was a historic agreement to create an Asbestos Claims Facility to be financed by subscribing insurers and producers, a facility endorsed in principle by numerous producers, including Manville. Through this facility, not yet operational at press time, participants hope that claims will be processed and paid expeditiously and without high administrative overhead, thus avoiding the courts altogether for at least several thousand of these troublesome cases. If this comes to pass, it will be a major achievement, made possible only through patient and dogged mediation. Without it, the asbestos cases will surely drag on through the courts to the end of this century and beyond.

Perhaps because people have read about mediation that helps solve high-charged, convoluted, complex, multiparty disputes like those involved in the Iranian hostage situation or the asbestos litigation, they tend to infer that mediation is useful only in a "megadispute." But mediation can be useful in almost any business quarrel.

The mediation of a shopping center dispute shows the possibilities. In 1983, the owner of a Virginia shopping center sought approval to develop vacant parcels, including highway frontage, for a gas station and convenience store. Three groups were opposed. Neighbors and town officials vehemently objected, among other things fearing a worsening of already heavily congested traffic at the site. The owners of adjacent townhouses had earlier formed the Haymarket Square Homes Association, which had succeeded in forcing a prior owner of the shopping center to remove a parking lot and repave a large area that had been improperly installed above the elevation permitted by the zoning plan. And provisions in the shopping center deeds gave authority to approve or deny design changes to the Hethwood Foundation, which represented 6,000 residents and a corporation that owned many apartment buildings in town. Hethwood vetoed the shopping center's proposal.

The shopping center owners pressed their zoning application, knowing that if they had a chance to succeed, it would only be in the Virginia courts. The town was apprehensive because its master zoning plan had never been tested in court. By the same token, the foundation was concerned about the possible financial failure of the shopping center, since it was important to the local economy.

At that point, the town suggested mediation and contacted the nearby Institute for Environmental Negotiation, a nonprofit organization affiliated with the University of Virginia. As part of the preliminary negotiations among the parties, each agreed, as the price of proceeding with the mediation:

1. That the town would not delay permit processing, even if the ultimate negotiated site plan turned out to be different.
2. That the chairman of the town planning commission and two staff members would participate actively in the negotiations.
3. That the shopping center owner would negotiate uses of all parcels in the shopping center, not just the parcel involving the gas station.
4. That the townhouse owners would support publicly any plan that the mediator helped negotiate to the satisfaction of all.
5. That the foundation would actively negotiate and not veto whatever it and the other parties agreed to.

During the next five weeks, five negotiating sessions were held at which the mediator developed a series of tradeoffs with which each party could live. Among the provisions in the comprehensive settlement were these: operating hours for the entire shopping center, specific separate operating hours for the gas station, access to the gas station from the major highway, and prohibition of left turns at the access. This kind of comprehensive settlement would probably not have succeeded without mediation. Each party was initially pursuing its own interest; the mediator helped the parties understand that each must weigh all the interests to resolve the dispute in a manner that would stand up over the long run. He succeeded; no lawsuit was ever filed.

But even for relatively simple two-party disputes, managers and their lawyers ought to consider the utility of mediators at the outset. Disputants rarely march directly to court; most defendants know for some time that a potential plaintiff is unhappy and that unless something is done a lawsuit will be filed. This is the time—when it is obvious a dispute cannot be settled immediately with a phone call—that a mediator can be most useful.

8

ARBITRATING DISPUTES

Advantages and Disadvantages

Arbitration is today probably the best-known and most highly organized alternative to the courtroom. Its use in resolving labor disputes is the frequent stuff of headlines. Arbitration flourishes in every area of the United States, through the twenty-six regional offices of the American Arbitration Association (AAA), through numerous ad hoc programs such as those offered by certain manufacturer groups and Better Business Bureaus, and through many other local, state, regional, and national trade associations. Beyond these programs, disputants often choose to arbitrate privately under their own rules.

Despite its widespread use, arbitration has not proved a panacea. Even the American Arbitration Association, which has long touted arbitration as *the* alternative, has lately begun to broaden the range of services it offers, in at least tacit recognition that arbitration is not always the most effective way to proceed. Arbitration is nonetheless an important form of dispute resolution, and one worth taking a closer look at here.

Arbitration is a kind of *adjudication*, the process of deciding by submitting a dispute to a third-party, neutral decision-maker with the authority to issue a *binding* judgment. For that reason, arbitration is not far removed from the adversary characteristics of litigation.

Disputants can look to arbitration to resolve their quarrels

in one of two distinct ways. If they have a contractual relationship, they can provide in the contract for arbitration as
the exclusive means of resolving any future dispute that arises
out of the contract. (For one such standard provision, see
Appendix C.) And whether or not the parties have a contract,
they can choose to submit to arbitration after the fact, once
the dispute is upon them.

That choice is binding in virtually every case. Federal law
and most state laws give absolute priority to arbitration hearings, so that any attempt to file a lawsuit will be stymied once
the arbitration process has begun. Should one party sue in the
face of a contract provision calling for arbitration, the other
party can easily obtain a stay of the lawsuit to permit the
arbitration to go forward. Nor is that the extent of the legal
protection given to arbitration. Once an arbitrator has handed
down an award, it can be entered in the court records and be
enforced as if it were an official court judgment. Moreover,
the arbitrator's award is not appealable, except under rare
circumstances (consequently, stenographic records of the proceedings are rarely kept). In any event, the parties may keep
the proceedings strictly confidential and closed to the press
and the outside world.

Three other features of arbitration mark it as different
from litigation. The hearing may be held wherever and whenever the parties agree. (If they agree in their contract to abide
by the rules of the American Arbitration Association, however,
they will be implicitly agreeing to hold the hearing in an AAA
hearing room at a time set by the arbitrator.) The rules of
proceeding at the hearing itself are extremely informal; the
rules of evidence, required in all courts, are not followed in
arbitration. Finally, the arbitrator is not selected randomly to
hear the case, as are judges; the parties may select any
arbitrator they wish, or provide by agreement for some other
means of choosing one (for example, from among a list provided
by the AAA).

Taken together, the seven features that follow make the

arbitration process, in theory at least, a quicker, cheaper, and better alternative to adjudication: (1) priority of arbitration over lawsuits, (2) enforcement of an arbitrator's award as if a judgment of a court, (3) nonappealability, (4) confidentiality, (5) time and place to suit the convenience of the parties, (6) informality of procedure, and (7) parties' choice of arbitrator.

We say that these features add up to lower costs, speed, and fairness *in theory*. In many cases, this is true. During the period from 1973 to 1983, the AAA handled on average more than 6,500 commercial arbitrations a year (exclusive of labor arbitrations). In smaller two-party cases calling for a single arbitrator to hear and resolve the dispute, the informality of the process can dispose in a morning of a case that might have taken days in court. But for many other cases, there is mounting evidence that arbitration is subject to many of the same difficulties that afflict the litigation process.

For example, some disputes are of a size and complexity that require a panel of arbitrators (under AAA rules and others). Scheduling difficulties can drag such a case on for as long as a lawsuit would take in a crowded court. Arbitrators are busy professionals—outside the labor field, few maintain a full-time practice as arbitrators. Finding dates on which all arbitrators can meet with the lawyers and parties can mean that hearings must be held in one-day chunks separated by perhaps months.

Like litigation, arbitration is an adversary process. Lawyers play much the same role they would in court, including conducting the extensive discovery often permitted under the arbitration rules. Although the hearing itself is simplified because the arbitrators do not follow formal rules of evidence, the pretrial work can be as costly and time-consuming as it is in litigation.

It is also frequently alleged that the incentive of the arbitrator is not necessarily to act as impartially as would a judge. Judges are not paid by the parties, and their jobs do not depend on deciding for one or the other. But at least for professional arbitrators, who depend on their reputations to be hired to hear future disputes, there is, it is said, a tendency to compromise so that no one will walk away in complete anger at the result, or else subtly to favor the party that is most likely to require arbitration again. (Since both parties must consent to a particular person's serving as arbitrator, the bias, if any, would have to be marginal; a person known to favor defendants, say, would not be likely to be hired by plaintiffs.)

It is hard to evaluate these criticisms in the field of general commercial arbitration. AAA arbitrators serve without fee unless the hearing lasts more than three days; the majority of arbitrations conclude before that. Hence, the incentive to "divide the baby" is much reduced, as is the desire to favor one side or the other in order to secure a renewed appointment. Moreover, the crucial fact to remember is that the laws providing for enforcement of the arbitrators' awards do not dictate the procedure to be used or the rules to be followed. As long as the process is arbitration—that is, as long as the parties agree beforehand to be bound by the arbitrator's award—they may devise any procedures they please for moving the process along. For example, they can provide sanctions for delay, and they can also seek out any arbitrator of their choosing. They can choose one who has never arbitrated before and is not likely to arbitrate again, so that they need have no fear that the arbitrator will favor one side or the other to obtain future assignments.

Procedures

Although the parties may create their own procedures (for an example of a specially tailored arbitration forum, see Appendix D), it will be useful to sketch the general AAA procedure.

The complainant notifies the AAA regional office that it is seeking an arbitration (as provided, say, in a contract with the party, known as the respondent, against whom the complainant has a grievance). The AAA will notify the respondent that an arbitration has been demanded, and will send each party a list of several names of potential arbitrators from a master file. (The AAA lists are divided by specialties—textiles, manufacturing, publishing, and so on. Those on the list are lawyer volunteers with some expertise in the particular area.) The parties are given the opportunity to agree on a particular arbitrator (or panel, if required). If they fail to agree, the AAA will pick the arbitrator from those on the supplied list. Likewise, the parties will be given the opportunity to specify the time and date of the arbitration; but if they cannot agree, the arbitrator is empowered to specify the timing. The hearing will ordinarily be held at an AAA office.

Depending on the complexity of the case, the arbitrator may ask for documents and briefs in advance of the hearing, and may permit the parties to conduct discovery. Disputes about prehearing matters are within the discretion of the arbitrator to decide.

The hearing is usually conducted around a large table. The parties may, and usually do, present their cases through their lawyers. The complainant first states its case and offers any evidence in the form of documents or witnesses. Although the lawyers may object to certain documents or statements, the arbitrators will ordinarily agree to hear whatever is proffered, since no formal rules of evidence are in force. Cross-examination is within the discretion of the arbitrator. The same informality applies to the respondent's presentation.

Although the procedures are informal, the arbitrator is bound to apply the law as it exists to the facts in the case; he or she is also bound by the power granted the arbitrator in the contract. The arbitrator may not decide matters between the parties that lie outside the contract or that were not raised in the papers filed with the AAA. An arbitrator who usurps power beyond that granted in the contract risks an appeal, one of the rare instances in which judicial review is allowed.

Within thirty days of the hearing's close, the arbitrator is bound to issue a ruling and an award, if any. He or she is not required to issue a written opinion. Both parties receive notification of the ruling and the award. The winning party will submit the arbitrator's award to the local court for entry on its records as a judgment. At that point, the case is over. Should the losing party fail to abide by the judgment (to pay the winner a specified amount of money), the winning party may seek enforcement just as if it had won in court.

Final Offer Arbitration

One relatively new variant of conventional arbitration is the so-called final offer arbitration. It is an ingenious device, used so far mostly in the labor field, to give greater incentives to the parties to do hard bargaining in the hope of heading off the hearing altogether.

In final offer arbitration, each party submits to the arbitrator a proposal for settling the dispute. The arbitrator considers each proposal at a hearing. The arbitrator may then choose one proposal or the other, but nothing else. He or she is forbidden from issuing a compromise award, and may not deviate at all from the proposal chosen as the final award.

In ordinary arbitration, the parties have an incentive to inflate their claims and demands, in the expectation that the arbitrator will compromise or average the claimant's highs and the respondent's lows. Given the tendency to inflate, the parties have little incentive to bargain. By contrast, in final offer arbitration the incentives are reversed. A demand that is too high will be rejected in favor of the more reasonable one, and the party making the unreasonable offer will lose all. So the tendency will be to make claims and demands that move toward the center. Precisely because of this tendency, the parties before the arbitration will have an even stronger incentive to bargain between themselves in an effort to avoid the risk of losing altogether. In the few states in which final offer arbitration has been adopted for use in labor and public employee disputes (it has also been used in major league baseball to settle salary disputes), experience suggests that the system works as designed, and dramatically reduces the number of cases that actually go to arbitration.

"Rent-a-Judge": Using Private Judges to Decide Disputes

A far less well-known variant of arbitration is "trial by reference," or, as the *Wall Street Journal* has dubbed it, trial by "rent-a-judge." All states except Illinois and Louisiana permit cases to be submitted to a "referee," a private individual not employed by the court system. (The federal court rules permit reference as well.) Although some states permit only certain issues to be referred and other states limit the effect of the referee's ruling, the variants all have in common that litigants may escape the crowded dockets of the local courts and maintain the confidentiality of the proceedings, while preserving the advantages of the legal rules of the courts.

In particular, California and New York, along with eight other states, have exceedingly liberal rules for trial by reference. The referee has authority to determine all issues of fact and law, and the decision is treated as if it were a jury verdict or the judgment of a trial court. This might sound like arbitration; indeed, it is close. The major differences are that the referee is bound to apply the rules of evidence and to follow other procedural rules and that the decision may be appealed to an appellate court. (In California, the parties may even consent to eliminate most formal rules of evidence and procedure.)

Unlike an ordinary trial, the rent-a-judge hearing may be conducted, like arbitration, in the offices of one of the parties, of the referee, or on neutral ground, at any time that is convenient. Because the referee—virtually all are retired judges—does not have a crowded docket, the case can be heard with dispatch, and the referee can be required to render a decision within a stipulated time. Once the decision is rendered, it is entered as a judgment in the court, and is therefore available to the press. But the documents that would have been available had this been a regular trial will not be open to the public, unless they are made part of a record on appeal. As a practical matter, in most appeals the parties stipulate to the record and do not submit many actual documents.

The major advantages of rent-a-judge proceedings are speed and the lower costs associated with quicker trials. (Unlike regular trials, however, the parties will pay the referee's fee, just as they pay the fee of a neutral advisor in a minitrial; see Chapters 3 and 4.) Another important advantage is that the parties can choose the particular judge and are not left to the random drawing that determines the judge in trial court. By choosing a judge familiar with the law and subject of the case, the parties can save further costs because they will not need to devote time to educating the judge; moreover, a judge familiar with the material will be less likely to commit appealable errors. Finally, to the extent that the parties wish to avoid the possible tendency of an arbitrator to compromise an award, they will benefit by having an experienced judge ruling on the law, and subject to appeal.

Laws providing for rent-a-judge trials have been around for a long time (California's statute is over a century old). But not until recently have these laws been dusted off. Apparently, the first modern application of the California rent-a-judge procedure was in 1976. Since then, more than 100 cases have been decided in such forums in Los Angeles alone. There seems little doubt that trial by referee can save—because it has saved—weeks or months of court time and hundreds of thousands of dollars in court costs.

It should be clear from all that has been said about the minitrial, mediation, and arbitration in all their forms that one skill underlies dispute resolution generally—negotiation. No matter who is hired to nudge the parties along or even to sit in eventual judgment, the parties themselves have a major responsibility for bringing their dispute to a close. In recent years much has been written about negotiation, to which we now turn.

9

NEGOTIATING SETTLEMENTS

A voluminous literature has recently sprouted on the theory and practice of negotiation. Within just a few years, the best-seller lists have swung from popular guides advocating ruthless toughness to more subtle guides emphasizing cooperation and compromise. It should be no surprise that Americans are fascinated with negotiation, because we are such an active society, ready to make deals and do business with one another daily. Yet our need to read about it suggests a fear that we are not negotiating as effectively as possible.

Professional managers today probably lead the country in their understanding and practice of negotiation and its critically related skill, communication. Few successful managers can have achieved their positions without having mastered the art of negotiating—with colleagues, superiors, subordinates, customers, suppliers, accountants, lawyers, government officials—in short, with all the people who contribute to the running of their business. Indeed, our entire economic enterprise would be impossible if it were not for the ability of managers (and many others, of course) to conduct the literally millions of negotiations daily that keep the nation free, strong, and wealthy.

Nevertheless, many of the most successful business negotiators have neglected one area in which they might usefully bring their skills to bear: negotiating an end to disputes. Even though the underlying essence of alternative approaches to dispute resolution is highly effective communication and negotiation, managers routinely hand over disputes lock, stock, and barrel to their lawyers, without considering whether they might themselves contribute to the settlement.

That they do is particularly surprising because of what happens when a dispute is put in the laps of the lawyers—not all lawyers, to be sure, but many of them. The lawyer, trained in adversary behavior, instinctively views the dispute as a battle to be won, rather than a problem to be solved, and the opposing party as the enemy, rather than a potential partner. If this picture is overbroad, it makes a significant point: Lawyers tend to see their job as combative rather than cooperative. This attitude adversely affects their attempts to settle lawsuits—what most lawyers end up doing most of the time with most disputes (recall that some 94 percent of all lawsuits are eventually settled without trial).

It surely is no coincidence that at the very time new dispute resolution techniques are being pioneered, scholars have developed a new understanding of negotiation and some new and improved techniques that anyone can use in negotiating.

The Adversary Approach or Positional Bargaining

To understand them, let us look at the basic adversary approach that lawyers (and many business executives) take to settling disputes. In two words, that approach is *maximize victory.* Assuming that both sides are playing this same negotiation "game," the process unfolds in four steps. First, each party sets for itself a "target": what it would like to gain from the negotiation. This target level is aspirational; it is usually (though not always) stated as the party's ideal ($1 million, a royalty-free patent license).

Second, each party will set its "reservation point," the point below (or above) which it will not settle—the point at which the party would rather risk going to court. The reservation point ordinarily is not disclosed to the adversary.

Third, the parties then engage in a virtual ritual of offer and counteroffer. This duel of offers is how most people think of negotiation. But it is meaningless without the first two steps. And the ritual itself is more often than not just that—a stylized manner of dealing with each other (when it is not an out-and-out sham). No one expects the other party to yield on hearing the first offer; a counteroffer is anticipated and dealt with by a new offer. The parties are testing each other, trying to ferret out the opponent's reservation point.

Fourth and finally, the parties discover some zone in which their target levels overlap, permitting them to settle for what to all the world seems to be some variant of "splitting the difference."

When disputants in a particular case argue over one issue only, this adversary negotiation process makes some sense. This is a "zero-sum" game, in which whatever one person gets the other must necessarily lose. Suppose a buyer has purchased a product and has disposed of it but has not fully paid the seller. (The buyer, a wholesaler, has complained that the product was substandard and that he could not get his expected resale price.) Suppose further that neither party expects to be doing business with the other in the future. The only issue is the amount owed. The seller concludes that it will be too expensive to seek redress in the courts, so he attempts to negotiate the amount to be paid. In such a situation, we might reasonably expect that the parties will tend to divide—the seller will get less than he demands but more than the buyer presumably wanted to pay.

The adversary approach to negotiation is simplistic. It assumes either that all situations are one-dimensional or that multidimensional problems can be satisfactorily negotiated through the adversary process. Neither assumption is correct. Few problems are so narrow that only one issue is important. Few cases are so simple that the parties cannot find potential tradeoffs to discuss. When many issues are at stake, the adversary approach often simply makes things worse.

There are a number of reasons why this is so. For one thing, a negotiator who is intent on achieving a particular goal (offer, counteroffer, or even a more tentatively expressed proposal) will be tempted to ignore alternatives which lie beyond the form in which he has expressed that objective. In this situation negotiators may find themselves, like a high school debater, giving all sorts of reasons why the adversary should accept the offer, without really listening to what the other party is saying, and thus forfeiting the chance to concentrate on what might be a different, but better, solution.

Adversary negotiation can result in no solution. If both sides are experienced adversary negotiators, their attempts to bluff, stonewall, and prod each other may lead to a withdrawal from negotiation and a subsequent showdown in court. Moreover, even if one side bullies the other into submission, the "loser" might resent the tactics and outcome sufficiently that it will ultimately not comply with the agreement—the loser might seek ways to circumvent it or even repudiate the bargain, forcing the "winner" to go to court anyway.

A further consideration arises because so often it is a lawyer who serves as the client's principal negotiator. Lawyers think in terms of the law, and they understand the law to mean what the court would award if a judge or jury were to decide the case. In the words of Professor Carrie Menkel-Meadow of the UCLA Law School, they are bargaining "in the shadow of the court." But thinking only in terms of the law and the courtroom is to lock oneself unnecessarily into a "legal" solution, instead of a resolution that might be far more congenial to the client. Furthermore, the legal solution is usually seen as "winner take all," because that is usually the only kind of solution a court can provide.

Even when a range within which to compromise is possible in court (for example, in a personal injury case when the jury can adjust the damage award), the negotiators who bargain in the shadow of the court set their targets and reservation points in accordance with what they presume they could get from the court. So negotiations outside court frequently turn on assertions of the defendant's lawyer that "you'd never get that in court" and the plaintiff's lawyer's response that "we could get a lot more than that in court." Since the parties are not in court and are seeking to avoid court, the negotiation is shallow and fails to take advantage of the full range of possible solutions.

To summarize, the difficulty with the adversary approach to resolving legal disputes through negotiation is threefold: (1) Assuming that they are dealing with single issues, the negotiators neglect other needs (and conceivably far more important needs) that the parties might have. (2) They also neglect the long-run consequences of the negotiated agreement (a "tough" agreement may deter one from doing business again with the other). (3) They may wind up with a stalemate, and hence no resolution, forcing them to court, possibly burdened by more anger and distrust than had they never initially negotiated.

Problem-Solving or Interest-Based Negotiation

The alternative to the adversary approach has several names. Professor Menkel-Meadow calls it the "problem-solving" approach. Roger Fisher and William Ury, in their best-selling book *Getting to Yes,* call it "principled" negotiation, or negotiation based on interests rather than positions. Whatever it is called, the concept is clear, though demanding: Concentrate on solving a problem rather than on winning.

Consider the often-cited example of Israel and Egypt bargaining in 1978 over the Sinai peninsula. Egypt wanted the territory returned to its control. Israel refused to return to the *status quo ante.* These were *positions:* (1) We must have all the land. (2) You can't have any of the land. The adversary approach would be to divide up the land in some compromise— perhaps the southwestern portion for Egypt, the northeastern portion for Israel. But the adversary result was in fact stalemate, since the compromise position was agreeable to neither. This

seemed like a zero-sum problem, until the parties were goaded
into looking through their positions and identifying their true
interests. At Camp David it turned out that these interests
were after all compatible, not mutually exclusive. Egypt wanted
sovereignty over its former territory; Israel wanted security
from invasion. Once the underlying interests were perceived,
fashioning a deal was suddenly within their grasp. In exchange
for Israel's return of full sovereignty over the land, Egypt
agreed to demilitarize the region, keeping its tanks and military
forces out.

Or consider this simple lawsuit example, the lessons of
which have been widely learned during the past few years by
insurance companies and plaintiffs' lawyers. In a typical case,
a plaintiff will have been seriously injured by the alleged
negligence of the defendant driver. The plaintiff's injuries will
arouse the jury's sympathies, but the defendant might be able
to create doubt about whether he or she in fact had acted
negligently. (Or perhaps the plaintiff was negligent also—
meaning that money damages would be eliminated or greatly
reduced.) The parties thus wish to avoid the risk of trial. Now
if they follow the adversary approach to negotiation, the
discussion between the lawyers will sound as if they were in
the courtroom all along. ("A jury would award us a million
dollars." "Yes, but I could convince them that your client was
negligent and in any event I would upset the verdict on
appeal.")

The problem-solving approach results in what has come
to be known as a *structured settlement.* Rather than paying
the plaintiff the total sum a jury would award at a single time,
the defendant (usually an insurance company) agrees to pay
out a smaller sum periodically. Here the mutual interests of
both parties are recognized—the defendant to pay less up
front, the plaintiff to recover for losses in a way that makes
economic sense. Sensible structured settlements are possible
in direct negotiations between parties who are disposed to
match their interests. The parties are not likely to arrive at

such comprehensive and mutually rewarding solutions in the heat of the courtroom or from the narrowness of a jury verdict.

Problem-solving negotiation requires more "brainwork" by the negotiators than adversary negotiation, in which each may assume he is doing his job simply by being stubborn. The negotiator first must seriously confront, with the client, the true problem: What are our *real* interests? What do we really want, as opposed to the position that we could, for the sake of convenience, assert to the other side? Both negotiator and client must overcome the understandable desire to "trounce" the other side; they must come to understand that quietly satisfying the underlying need is far more important than defeating the adversary with flags flying. It is not a defeat for one if both mutually gain. (This is not to say that every conceivable dispute will be amenable to such constructive results. A person who believes she has been libeled in a newspaper may earnestly desire vindication in the same forum in which she was libeled. But the newspaper just as strenuously may resist correcting the record—at least in the same form in which the defamation was arguably committed.)

Discussions between client and lawyer-negotiator obviously cannot exhaust the process of finding the best solution. They will have to talk to the other side. A negotiation must be a dialogue, presented as such, in which each side seeks to construct the largest mutual gain. The parties cannot do this if they seek only to maximize victory for themselves. Too much will be omitted from the discussion. Instead, each needs to have thought through questions it should be asking the other, in order to ascertain where everyone's true interest lies. This process, if done well, will closely resemble a business brainstorming session, in which people seek to articulate as many alternatives as possible without feeling that by making a suggestion they are either subject to ridicule or locked into accepting it.

As we readily admit, the problem-solving approach will not always yield results. Disparities of power may reduce the incentive of the powerful to bargain at all. Some bargaining situations surely are zero-sum. Sometimes the plaintiff will want the defendant punished or forced to acknowledge fault, and that demand will be nonnegotiable. But even if these factors are present in some degree, an attempt to use the problem-solving approach may be rewarded, and in the huge majority of cases these factors simply are of no account.

Negotiating Styles

So far we have been concerned with an approach toward negotiating. We have not talked about the particular personality of the negotiator or the style he or she uses in negotiating. The subject is worth a brief look primarily to debunk the common belief that the approach to negotiation dictates the style in which the negotiation is undertaken.

It is conventional to view negotiating styles as polar opposites—as either hard or soft. Many people believe that an adversary approach means an aggressive style, and that a problem-solving, cooperative approach means a weak style. In fact, there is no necessary correlation between the personal style of the negotiator and the negotiating approach taken. Moreover, research on the effect of personality on outcomes suggests that either the "hard" or "soft" style can produce results if competently employed. A study by Professor Gerald R. Williams of Brigham Young Law School has more usefully labeled as "cooperative" and "competitive" the two basic negotiating styles of lawyers. The effective cooperative style is marked by these characteristics: trustworthiness, courtesy, cooperation, and legal astuteness. The effective cooperative negotiator is also perceptive in reading the opponent's cues and is an effective and convincing trial attorney. By contrast, the ineffective cooperative negotiator, while sharing many of the personality characteristics just listed, is too trustful of others and overly obliging. He rates getting along with the opponent more highly than does the effective cooperator.

The aggressive style is marked by a forceful or dominating personality who is not afraid to make high opening demands, and who cleverly exploits whatever openings he or she can find. This person is likewise a convincing and effective trial attorney, skillful at reading an opponent's cues. He makes a point of getting to know the opponents, but despite what some of these characteristics may connote, the effective aggressive negotiator is honest and ethical. By contrast, the ineffective aggressive negotiator has all the negative characteristics commonly associated with the style: He is irritating, unreasonable, demanding, argumentative, quarrelsome, withholds information when it is unnecessary to do so, and puts propositions on a take-it-or-leave-it basis. This person is headstrong—rigid and egotistical. He is also arrogant, uninterested in the needs of others, if not downright intolerant, and frequently hostile.

It should be no surprise that an overly cautious or overly aggressive negotiator will be ineffective. It might come as a surprise that negotiators, whether they follow an adversary or problem-solving approach, can be effective with either a cooperative or a competitive style. Although much research remains to be done, it seems a plausible conclusion at this point that personal style, though certainly not unimportant, is less important to the outcome than the substantive approach the negotiator takes to the problem.

Nor are the cooperative and competitive styles necessarily the only ones. Fisher and Ury contrast what they term the "soft" and "hard" bargainers with "principled" bargainers. The soft bargainer makes concessions to cultivate the relationship; the hard bargainer demands concessions as a condition of the relationship. The soft bargainer trusts others; the hard bargainer trusts no one. The soft bargainer searches for agreements the other side will accept; the hard bargainer searches for an agreement he or she can accept. The soft bargainer tries to avoid a contest of wills; the hard bargainer tries to win a contest of wills. In comparison, the principled negotiator eschews these polar extremes. He avoids making demands or yielding to them; he separates the people—the negotiators—from the problem they are negotiating. He proceeds independently of trust, neither swayed nor deterred by its presence or absence. The principled negotiator develops multiple options, avoids making quick decisions, and searches for standards other than will on which to base a judgment.

What happens when a cooperative negotiator meets a competitive bargainer, or a hard bargainer meets a principled one? Experienced negotiators will have their own answers, no doubt, but current research tends to suggest that the worst move is for a problem-solving negotiator to adopt an adversary approach, confusing it with an aggressive style. The principled negotiator, the one committed to a search for solutions to a problem rather than to standing and winning on a position, will refuse to play the other's game, for that way lies little likelihood of success. In time, maintaining the problem-solving posture, whatever the style, may bring the opponent around.

What is the manager's role in all this? We have suggested throughout this book that the executive must take a greater part in the resolution of the disputes that affect the company. For the sake of convenience and efficiency, it may continue to make sense to turn disputes over to the legal staff for resolution (and they in turn may hand the disputes on to outside counsel). But such disposition should not be undertaken without reviewing the approaches and methods of the lawyers. If you sit down with them initially, before the first phone call is made to the opposition, and explore the options, giving them directions, brainstorming the possible outcomes, and identifying the interests at stake, they will not only infer the need to become problem-solving negotiators, they will also learn how to do it. Taking the time and trouble to do this will measurably improve the outcome.

10

HOW TO FIND
A NEUTRAL

As we have seen, one of the keys to avoiding courtroom litigation is the creative use of a neutral—as third-party advisor in a minitrial, as mediator, as arbitrator, or in some other process. But neutrals do not—at least not yet—advertise as such. (A few mediation services, exclusively in the family law area, do advertise now in the Yellow Pages. But these are not likely to be suitable for business disputes.) How, then, can you go about looking for one? Where can you find a neutral?

Happily, America is a nation rich in just this resource. Tens of thousands of people throughout the country can be called on to perform the neutral's function. Once we recognize that potential neutrals are all around us, the problem is to identify a person with the qualities needed to resolve a particular dispute.

Most of us at one time or another have acted as a neutral—in mediating a dispute among children, colleagues, or among two guests at the dinner table on Saturday night when they became a little too heated over sports, religion, or politics. So ingrained is this peace-making activity that we often do not think of it when the need for it arises in more formal contexts. Yet many highly able people at the heads of corporations and other enterprises, in law firms and in academe have the skills to play the role of a formal neutral in a private dispute resolution process.

One source of such people is the panels various dispute resolution services have assembled. One such is the Judicial Panel of the Center for Public Resources. Another is the mediation panel of the American Arbitration Association. Others are being formed by bar groups in major metropolitan areas across the country, examples being the Federal Bar Panel in New York City and the dispute resolution program of the Denver City Bar. Several law schools have begun to sponsor dispute resolution services, including those at Duke in North Carolina and the University of California at San Diego. In addition to these groups, all of which are not for profit, for-profit businesses have begun to provide dispute resolution services. Perhaps the most well-known is EnDispute, Inc., headquartered in Washington, D.C.

To illustrate how these various groups work, we will take a brief look at CPR's Judicial Panel. Funded in large part by a grant from the Aetna Life & Casualty Foundation, the Judicial Panel was established in 1982 to foster three goals: (1) to promote alternative dispute resolution, (2) to expand the frontiers of dispute resolution in the corporate and institutional arena, and (3) to demonstrate the richness of such resources in the United States.

Panel members all have extensive legal and business experience. Many are retired or former federal or state judges; several have experience as CEOs of businesses, as deans and academic heads, as diplomats, and as federal cabinet officers and heads of administrative agencies. All are well known within the legal community; most are nationally known outside the legal community. (An updated list of members is available from CPR.)

The hallmark of the panel is its flexibility. Participation is purely voluntary, and the members stand ready to help disputants through a minitrial, mediation, arbitration, or other privately negotiated process. Because the proceedings of the panel are confidential, unless the parties agree to release the results, no published statistics are available to indicate how frequently panel members are called on to serve as neutrals, or how often their services have led to a successful resolution. Nevertheless, we can describe the general process by which a panel member is engaged.

The most frequent method of engaging the services of the panel is by calling CPR for a consultation on which panel member is most suited, geographically and by specialty and temperament, to serve as a neutral in the specific dispute in which the caller is involved. If the parties agree to initiate discussions with the neutral, CPR will put the panel member in touch with the disputants. Initial talks will focus on the type of process that is most likely to meet the needs of the parties and on the role that the neutral can most sensibly play. The initial talks are important also as a means of outlining the areas of agreement and trust that exist at the outset. A neutral who participates in these initial talks can help narrow the issues from the outset and set the stage for a cooperative rather than a hostile encounter. As the talks progress (and these can be one or two half-day meetings), the ground rules will be drawn up and the process will be put into motion.

Perhaps the most publicized efforts of the Judicial Panel were the so-called Wellington negotiations to establish the Asbestos Claims Facility (see Chapter 7). To underscore what has already been said, one important reason for the success to date of those negotiations is that they took place on neutral ground, in an atmosphere in which all parties, no matter how much they might disagree among themselves on any specific issue, found themselves driven to find an area of mutual accommodation.

But just as no disputant or potential disputant needs to be tied to one type of process for resolving disputes, so the disputant need not be locked into one particular source of neutrals, whether it be CPR's Judicial Panel or any other. Any community, even a relatively tiny one, has a reservoir of talent that can serve this function. If they are disposed to find a nonlitigious way out of a pending dispute, two companies might well make it the first order of business to sit down and discuss where they might search for a neutral to help recommend the type of resolution process to use. Among the people to search for and places to look are these: retired judges,

CEOs of local companies (and retired CEOs), the general counsel of a company in the area that is uninvolved in the dispute, the dean of the local law school or certain law school professors who have had some experience in negotiation (for example, teachers of labor law, mediation, and the like), and other administrators and community leaders with a reputation for impartiality and levelheadedness.

Of course, not everyone who appears on the surface to be suitable as a neutral will in fact be so. Early experience in this arena suggests at least some tentative guidelines to follow in choosing suitable candidates. To begin with, the ideal neutral should have legal experience. That probably means, at this juncture in the evolution of dispute resolution, that the neutral should be a lawyer. Cynics beware: This is not a backdoor approach to hiring unemployed litigators. Let us make it clear why legal training is almost certainly a requirement for serving as a neutral in most business disputes of even moderate complexity.

No business dispute beyond the most trivial can be understood outside the legal environment in which it is enmeshed. Whether it involves contract law, negligence, or federal or state regulations governing virtually every aspect of business, the dispute has a legal component that cannot be disregarded. A neutral, who must be alert to every nuance of the dispute, cannot afford to be ignorant of the important legal nuances. For example, in the area of employee hiring and firing, the law is undergoing vast and fairly rapid change in most states. To be able to assess a particular dispute, it is not enough to understand the facts alleged to be at issue; it is also crucial to understand them against the backdrop of a changing legal scene. The mediator or minitrial neutral advisor who could not take into account the *probability* that the courts might deviate from past decisions would not be doing the job well. The person most likely to possess this kind of knowledge is, of course, the lawyer.

But not just any lawyer will do. Those who have spent

their entire careers as litigators, to single out perhaps the largest class of people who might want to act as neutrals, very probably are not best suited to the role. As a class, they have developed adversary habits that make it difficult to play a demanding and quite different role. Far better is the lawyer who has had practical, hands-on experience as a dispute resolver in one or more different roles as judge, administrator, manager, corporate lawyer, negotiator, dean, or CEO. Since the law school dean may not seem an obvious choice, we suggest that such a person be considered: In addition to the requisite substantive legal knowledge, the dean will have an acute appreciation of the need to facilitate the resolution of disputes, and if he or she has been in the position for any length of time, will have developed skills for doing so. (Of course, law school deans are not plentiful; relative to the number of disputes they are exceedingly scarce, and they may be in no position to take the time to serve as a neutral.) We stress that we are not talking about second-rate men and women for the job of neutral. Anyone will *not* do. It must be the right person, chosen through the right panel, for the right process. Experience and skill are unquestionable prerequisites.

All this suggests that business leaders ought on their own to be developing sources from the potential neutrals who live and work in their communities. Since the role of neutral is quintessentially that of a private, unofficial problem-solver and dispute resolver, nothing prevents you, your company, your trade association, or other group or groups from creating your own panel or panels of neutrals. And since you will be looking for experienced people with a certain set of skills, it will take time. That is why you should begin before any particular dispute, or set of disputes, is on the horizon.

You can go about this task in a number of ways. A CEO or senior manager might wish personally to contact eligible neutrals—for example, retired judges and CEOs, academics, and community leaders. These discussions can be ad hoc and private, the goal simply to obtain a stated willingness on the part of these people to consider serving as neutrals should the occasion ever arise. Or the discussions can be public, in the sense that the prospective neutrals' willingness to participate might be recorded somewhere, so that others will know of their availability.

Similarly, a company, a trade association, or some other group might wish to put together its own panel of neutrals on a public basis. It can do so through its own contacts (members, customers) or through a public call, aided by stories in the local papers and by direct involvement of the law department and the public affairs staff. Such an endeavor should reap favorable publicity for any company that undertakes it. Moreover, the effort of putting together a list of eligible neutrals can foster a business climate that will induce others to spurn the courtroom when disputes arise. (This notion is in part behind the idea of the Public Pledge, now signed by some 100 major corporations, to try ADR rather than automatically litigate, when a dispute arises with another company that has signed the pledge. The pledge is discussed in more detail in Chapter 14.)

It might seem that it will be necessary to hunt high and low for a few willing to serve, to cajole the very few who will express interest. To the contrary, we believe that the major problem awaiting the compilation of a "neutrals panel" will be quality control: screening out the many who will come forth, eager but unfit to serve in the neutral role. Numerous lawyers and professional mediators from the field of family disputes will want to sign on, but the temptation to include all who apply must be resisted. The lawyer who claims to have had a psychology course in college but who has spent his professional life drafting wills or litigating in court is not, for reasons already given, ideal. Nor is the professional mediator whose entire experience is limited to the family arena. Business disputes are significantly different, and call for a body of knowledge unlikely to be the common possession of the nonlawyer, professional mediator.

Despite all the foregoing it is not true that all nonlawyers are unsuited to the role. A senior personnel administrator, for example, may have significant knowledge of employee relations law, and be sensitive to the nuances of the inner workings of a corporation. So it will be necessary for anyone compiling a list of neutrals first to evaluate the types of skills that fit the dispute profile of the company—a company that finds itself frequently contesting patents will want a different sort of panel from one that is embroiled in disputes with its large workforce.

We can't tell you exactly what your panel should look like; no formula is possible. And that is precisely the advantage of doing it yourself: You can tailor a panel to your specifications and those of your industry.

11

MANAGING THE LAW FUNCTION

Historically, the law department of the company has been left in the hands of the lawyers. The law function has seemed so specialized that few CEOs or senior managers have overseen its activities as they would the marketing department, or finance, or any other. In recent years, some CEOs and senior executives have come to see this attitude as misguided. The legal function of a corporation requires managerial oversight as much as, if not more than, many other corporate activities.

Many sophisticated companies have begun to do so by installing top-notch, experienced general counsel, who compare in every way to the best lawyers in well-known law firms. Although some corporations have had first-rate lawyers for a long time, in many companies the general counsel's position did not always seem to call for such a high-caliber person. For at least the past decade, however, more and more companies have brought in good lawyers, many with management experience, and put them to work building a sophisticated law department.

By the mid-1970s, these general counsel had begun to ask their outside lawyers some penetrating questions about the way they were practicing law on behalf of their clients. The overriding issue has been cost control. Costs have been addressed in a variety of ways: dealing in-house with many of the legal functions formerly delegated to outside law firms, careful scrutiny of bills, use of new billing techniques, litigation budgeting, and risk analysis. Many of the approaches to cost

95

control bear only indirectly on dispute resolution, but some of them are having a direct impact on the way companies go about resolving their disputes.

Litigation Budgeting

One tool, now being used by an increasing number of companies, is the *litigation budget*. It stems from the simple proposition, basic to all other corporate operations, that managers must think through their expenditures and budget for the task to be accomplished. No company would ever manufacture or market a product without preparing an elaborate budget; no corporate department runs without one, including the law department. Why not, then, a budget for lawsuits?

In the comparatively innocent days of the early 1970s and before, a company facing a lawsuit would typically turn over all the papers to its outside law firm. That firm would then begin to go through the motions of pretrial discovery: interrogatories, depositions, and demands for the production of documents. A number of associates would be briefed on the case, and they would turn to the work without much, if any, discussion about the payoff from deposing forty people, say, rather than twenty or ten or five, given the costs associated with each effort. The top inside lawyer would probably have asked the senior partner for a "ballpark" estimate of the litigation cost, and a single figure might have been given.

Today, no sophisticated company will proceed with litigation on such a seat-of-the-pants basis in any big lawsuit, and rarely will it do so even in smaller cases. Instead, the inside general counsel will want to see a detailed budget—and ought to see it on paper.

The initial budget will provide the first best guess about the level of expenditures for personnel and for disbursements. It will pinpoint (1) the tasks to be performed, (2) the level or status of the people to do them (senior partner or junior associate), (3) the number of people, and (4) how long each task will take. The disbursements consist of travel, document copying, depositions, and the like. (For a sample litigation budget, see Appendix E.)

The numbers in the proposed budget are less important than that they be matched to categories of expenditures. For the purpose of the budget is to force both lawyers and managers to think hard about the steps to be taken in each particular lawsuit. How many depositions should be pursued? Of whom? What is the expected return from each? How many documents, and which ones, should be sought? Where are they likely to be found? How many people will it take to dig them out? What constitutes basic research in the case? What is peripheral? How detailed should the pleadings be? The briefs? From these questions, lawyers and managers will develop a far better understanding of the case and the expected return. Of course any first budget is preliminary, subject to revision as the lawyers learn more from the initial depositions and discoveries. Time enough then to revise as necessary. But the budget will always serve as the first tool for both lawyers and executives to manage the case.

That budgeting is essential does not mean that the budget will be the first topic of discussion between client and lawyers. For, as Richard McMillan, Jr., partner in the Washington law firm Crowell & Morning, notes: "It is unreasonable to expect outside counsel to come up with a meaningful budget when he has had only a few hours familiarity with your case. And it is misleading to the client. The outside lawyer simply doesn't know enough at the start of most cases to make a reasonable estimate; and clients who assume otherwise, and rely on the numbers they receive, are managing by faith alone." McMillan compares litigation to mining: The prospector must study the ground before saying just where to drill. So too must the lawyer research the case before deciding how best to proceed and to budget for it. And, says McMillan, "If a client will allow me these extra weeks to establish a budget, I am prepared to give him something in return—greater accountability to that budget. Once a reasonable budget is established, it should provide the client with a mechanism to ensure better accountability. If the cost target is subsequently exceeded, outside counsel should be expected to provide a detailed explanation. Most lawyers should be willing to accept this greater level of accountability to the budget—if that budget has been carefully and fairly arrived at."

Litigation Risk Analysis

A related tool is *litigation risk analysis*. Many business executives are familiar with decision analysis and decision trees, common fare at most business schools. This same mode of analysis is now being applied to legal decision-making.

Although the details are complicated, the basic idea is simple enough. Every case calls on lawyers and managers to make dozens or hundreds (or in complex cases, thousands) of decisions. The most basic is whether to bring the case at all (or, in the defendant's shoes, whether to defend against it or instead concede liability and negotiate a settlement). Either of those decisions, in turn, is based on innumerable calculations about the probability and worth of prevailing and the costs of doing so. To pursue a suit (or to defend against it actively) requires a plan involving numerous factors: the breadth and depth of pretrial discovery, the number and types of lawyers to assign to the case, and the strategy to pursue at trial.

The lawyer's approach to such questions has been intuitive: a "gut" feeling about the types of discovery and the lengths to which it should be taken. This "gut" feeling is given direction by the vague instructions of the client: "We want to win this case no matter what the cost"; "This one isn't worth it, see what you can do"; "We think we have a chance to prevail, but don't spend too much doing it." Litigation risk analysis tries to overcome the vagueness by quantifying these "gut" feelings and ambiguous directions.

For example, the question whether to demand the production of documents at a defendant's branch headquarters should be susceptible to somewhat more precision than simply "why not?" When pressed, the supervising lawyer might venture the prediction that the chance of turning up relevant and useful information would be "good." Pressed further, he might suppose that that chance was in the neighborhood of 75 or 90 percent (or whatever). If every lawyer who said "good" translated that term into similar numbers, little would be gained from this exercise. But it is unfortunately true that, like most people, lawyers use such terms quite loosely. A "good" chance to one lawyer might mean nothing less than 90 percent, to another anything over 50 percent. So although the number in itself is not scientifically valid, it nevertheless will reflect a reasonable judgment by the lawyer who has seen other cases and other results. It therefore permits a far sounder decision to be made about whether or not to proceed with the costly discovery.

Once the lawyer has assessed the probability of achieving a particular objective by undertaking a particular task (demanding discovery of certain documents at branch headquarters), that number is factored into an increasingly elaborate "decision tree," similar to the decision trees used in making marketing and manufacturing decisions. Litigation risk analysis is complicated; but hundreds of lawyers have been taking training in risk analysis in the past few years because, properly used, it is a powerful tool in effectively and efficiently managing a company's litigation.

Other Cost Controls

The days are long gone when a lawyer could submit a bill that says "for services rendered." Since the early 1970s, law firms have been computerizing their billing information; they know what each associate and partner did with every minute of billable time. An increasing number of corporations are demanding to see that information. A company that fails to do so is wasting a valuable opportunity to monitor and help shape the way it responds to legal disputes. For example, if you have hired a law firm on the strength of a senior partner's reputation, it should interest you to know whether or not that senior partner is in fact working on the case; it should also interest you to know that lawyers at one firm seem to take twice as long as others to draft similar documents. Without the check of a detailed billing statement, the litigation budget is useless. Furthermore, close supervision and monitoring assure adherence to company objectives.

The billing statement will also permit you to make accurate comparisons between similar cases in which your company has been involved. Many companies are subject to repetitive types of legal actions. No company should waste the opportunity to build accurate cost histories. By comparing the record of actual disbursements in like cases, a company can assure itself that a current lawsuit is not getting out of hand (and that litigation, rather than an alternative, is the best means to settle the dispute).

Beyond straightforward changes in billing practices, companies can innovate in the way they assign cases or parts of cases. The Bank of America has begun to experiment by shipping discrete problems out to law firms for research. Typically, it will spend between $3,000 and $10,000 on a particular issue, usually a small aspect of a much larger lawsuit. When the research is completed, the law firm's involvement in the case ends. This program enables the bank's lawyers to obtain opinions on substantive issues—an objective assessment of a confused state of the law, for example, or a second opinion to corroborate internal work.

Another company, Aetna Life & Casualty Company, learned to reduce payments to outside counsel some 35 percent during the early 1980s, when other costs were soaring. According to Peter Mear, Aetna counsel, its success was due largely to its ability to resolve some 65 percent of its corporate litigation cases in the first three months without participation of outside counsel. It does so by focusing on what it terms "pre-process," rather than on the trial or formal dispute resolution processes. The pre-process consists of a quick but substantial investigation and analysis of the issues.

After securing an extension of time from the plaintiff's counsel, Aetna's legal staff, ordinarily its paralegals, investigates the case and writes up a fact summary. Documents are gathered, and key witnesses are interviewed. Preliminary estimates of liability and damages are undertaken. The pre-process has taught Aetna (and the lesson is presumably true for other companies) that it is not necessary to search for all the facts in order to reach settlement. Probably 80 to 90 percent of the relevant facts are available without formal discovery.

This process has also shown that, to set priorities and objectives early, in-house litigation counsel should always establish facts, locate documents, and fix the stories of witnesses immediately. The analysis should be in writing because it forces counsel to analyze the case more thoroughly and thus puts the lawyer in a better position to negotiate.

With the analysis, an Aetna lawyer then discusses the case with an appropriate executive who has settlement authority. Early involvement of the executive helps set corporate objectives, determines what course to follow, permits a narrowing of the scope of the dispute, and brings the executive into the process as ally and participant. At this point, Aetna will consider whether to negotiate directly or employ one of the ADR processes described in this book. If the opposing counsel refuses to negotiate or consent to an ADR process, none of the time has been wasted; Aetna is poised to approach the ensuing litigation far more efficiently than it otherwise would have been.

More ambitiously, a company can undertake to track how disputes arise within the organization and how they are handled before reaching the law department. This effort is only just underway in a few companies; it is uncharted territory in most. The subject is too large for extended treatment here, but a simple example should make the point.

One company had a rule that settlements of legal disputes made by department managers were chargeable against their budgets. If, on the other hand, the dispute were to remain unresolved, it would pass to the law department, where an eventual settlement or court judgment would not be charged to the operating unit in which it first arose. This was a recipe for buck-passing. The rational manager would find reasons for refusing to settle, not incidentally aggravating the dispute in the process. By the time the dispute arrived in the law department, litigation was almost a foregone conclusion, and the company, not the department manager, was the net loser.

By "mapping" the "dispute maturation process," in the words of Edward K. Hamilton, of the Los Angeles management consulting firm Hamilton, Rabinovitz & Szanton, Inc., the manager can learn where and how disputes are arising and how they are transformed—and at what cost—as they wend their way through the company. Having looked at the dispute maturation process in a number of businesses, Hamilton has concluded that, with the exception of major lawsuits, companies generally spend "much" more money on a dispute before it gets to the law department than the law department spends once a dispute has come before the lawyers for disposition.

The mapping process is important also because in developing the information necessary for a complete picture of how the company responds to disputes, it will reveal where disputes are repeatedly arising and will suggest ways in which the company might be able to prevent disputes in the first place. We turn next to the prospects for preventive law.

12

PREVENTIVE LAW

Disputes that never arise need never be settled. In the long run, learning to head off disputes by avoiding the accidents, disruptions, and actions that cause them is the most effective form of dispute resolution. In every other area of business, the manager tries not merely to react, but to build strategies for control. That ought to be done in the legal area as well. In some ways it is; indeed, many leading corporations are front-runners among preventive law practitioners. In these companies, the concept of dispute prevention has been around for a long time under different names. For example, most sizable companies have antitrust compliance programs designed to forestall conduct that could lead to charges of violating antitrust laws. Quality control, safety engineering, and warranting programs are all examples of ways companies can head off potential causes of lawsuits.

But business could do far more than it currently does to practice preventive law. The problem is that preventive law falls between the cracks, belonging to neither the inside law department nor the outside lawyers. It is up to senior management to ensure that the function is built into the company in whatever ways make sense for the particular corporation. In this chapter we consider four approaches to preventive practices.

The Legal Audit

To learn how and why your company becomes engaged in disputes, you ought to consider a *legal audit*. Just as accountants audit the corporate books to ensure that the business is financially shipshape, so outside lawyers can audit the legal affairs of the company.

A *litigation audit* will tell corporate officials in what ways it is vulnerable whenever it is sued. Vulnerability can arise from any number of factors. The company may save every scrap of paper, all subject to discovery when a lawsuit is filed. A sensible document retention policy—stating where and how long documents must be saved—can minimize the costs of discovery and some of the risks (both of saving and of discarding paper, for the laws cut both ways). It can also prevent documents from being taken out by departing employees nursing grievances against their former employers. No less important, a litigation audit will uncover certain markings routinely made that could be a flag for later trouble; for instance, notations like "destroy after reading" (in cases in which the admonition is ignored).

But a legal audit can be far broader than a strategy for minimizing vulnerability to litigation once it is filed. It can also, and far more importantly, be used to prevent litigation from ever arising. A legal audit can be used to determine corporate trouble spots, places that generate far more disputes than the law of averages dictates. A legal audit of this sort would build a statistical base to show how many disputes arise during the course of the year, the type of plaintiff and complaint, and the place or person within the company against whom the claim is being asserted. Meticulous recordkeeping will show that the manufacturing plant in Petaluma or the shipping station in Wayzata are causing a number of the incidents on which the disputes are based. If lawsuits are seen to be piling up because an employee is failing to follow instructions, or because the set of operating instructions in a particular endeavor are erroneous, the obvious thing to do is admonish the employee or rewrite the operating instructions.

Yet it is astonishing how rarely companies pause to consider why they are being sued and what they might do to prevent the litigation. That is because companies are in the habit of handing their disputes over to the lawyers, whose job is not defined to include statistical surveys of the sort called for in a legal audit.

Yet lawyers in some companies do survey their cases. In 1983, the law department of Bank of America established a preventive law log, a computerized effort to track lawyers' suggestions to managers. The log also contains lists of practices that carry the risk of possible continuing financial exposure noted by the lawyers in the course of handling various cases. The log is maintained and monitored by the litigators, who can then find the name of the manager to whom a particular suggestion has been offered. Through the log, the lawyer can contact the senior person in the area affected by the problem, request remedial action, and track the results.

Contractual Commitments to ADR

Contracting out of litigation—agreeing to pursue some other means of resolving a dispute—is another form of preventive law. We have already seen in Chapter 8 how easily companies may commit to arbitration with a single sentence in a contract (Appendix C). There is no reason to believe that arbitration clauses exhaust the usefulness of this device.

Why not put a minitrial provision in a contract? The obvious objection to such a clause is that a minitrial is a voluntary procedure and works only when the parties are willing to work together. A party that balks at arbitration can be forced to submit to the arbitrator's jurisdiction, but what does it mean to be ordered to take a case to a minitrial? Despite the drawback of nonenforceability, there is still a case to be made for a range of ADR clauses in contracts.

Consider a simple negotiate-in-good-faith clause. If the parties are genuinely determined not to negotiate, no court order will suffice to enforce it. But the very existence of such a clause can nudge the parties toward negotiation. For most people do not lightly disregard what they have contractually undertaken to perform, and senior executives might feel bound at least to talk, since they have nothing to lose but their voices.

These types of clauses are frequently used when the parties foresee the very real possibility of a dispute because they cannot find a way to deal with the issue at the time the agreement is drafted. Open-price terms, price changes, and products subject to license are among the kinds of subjects often governed by a negotiate-in-good-faith clause. Such a clause could name the specific executives who must meet to attempt to settle whenever a dispute arises. Naming names puts significant moral and institutional pressure on the executives to work diligently toward a settlement.

A related type of clause is the cooling-off provision. This provides that no lawsuit may be filed until thirty or sixty days or some other period of time has elapsed after notice of intention to file a suit. (It bars any suit from being filed if notice has not been given.) During the cooling-off period, the parties have the chance to negotiate their differences, and the clause might explicitly call on the parties to address the dispute face to face.

From such clauses it is no great leap to a contractual provision for a minitrial (for examples, see Appendix B). The contract can commit the parties to pursue ADR in good faith in the event of a dispute. In calling for a minitrial, the contract could spell out the details of the procedure to be followed, but that is not a prerequisite. The details can be left to the parties themselves to negotiate when the need arises. Only two elements are necessary to make it clear that the parties have agreed to attempt to resolve their dispute through a minitrial: They must agree to some sort of information exchange before executives with settlement authority, and the executives must attempt in good faith to negotiate a settlement after the hearing. (A stronger version of an agreement to conduct a minitrial would be a provision that commits the parties to hold a minitrial and negotiate, but that empowers the neutral advisor to issue a binding decision, should settlement fail. In effect, this is a cross between a minitrial and arbitration and would, we think, be enforceable as an agreement to arbitrate.)

Contract clauses specifying the use of ADR before going to arbitration or litigation are not yet common, but they should be, especially in contracts between parties who have had long-standing relationships or who anticipate that the deal they are making will initiate a solid relationship. Unlike the arbitration clause, clauses for the other range of ADR mechanisms—minitrial, mediation, direct good faith negotiation—are not binding and should not be seen as depriving the parties of any essential rights. The parties may always go to arbitration or court if they have to, but the clauses may make it possible for them to avoid it.

Consumer Appeals Boards

A number of companies have created internal consumer dispute resolution mechanisms. By pledging to submit a dispute to an appeals board, they hope to obviate the consumer's feeling that he or she has no recourse but to sue in court. An example is the Ford Motor Company's Consumer Appeals Board (FCAB) program. The twenty-nine boards hear disputes brought by Ford automobile owners; they do not hear matters already in litigation, sales problems, or personal injury or property damage claims.

The FCAB procedure is simplicity itself. The customer need only write the board in the state in which his or her dealer is located (boards exist in most states, but unfortunately not in all of them). A simple one-page form is available, to which the customer may attach whatever documents or statements he believes will be helpful. Each FCAB consists of five members: three consumer representatives, a Ford dealer, and a Lincoln-Mercury dealer. Oral arguments are by invitation of the board only. The board notifies the dealer, who submits a similar form to explain his side of the story. The boards meet monthly and decide most cases on the basis of the papers presented, although board members may inspect the vehicles if they desire. A majority vote decides the issue.

From the customer's perspective, the most important aspect of the FCAB program is that any decision against Ford or its dealers is binding, and no appeal is possible. Customers, on the other hand, are not bound by FCAB decisions; a losing customer may still go to court. If a dealer refuses to comply, Ford will stand in place of the dealer and offer financial assistance to the customer.

In 1984, the FCABs heard 11,000 cases and resolved some 3,800 in favor of customers. Dealer support for the FCAB program is reportedly high. And no wonder. Now in its eighth year, it stands as a particularly potent way to minimize or eliminate disputes that would otherwise be mired in court.

Neutral Fact-Finding and the Ombudsman

Any company of even modest size conducting a legal audit today would quickly discover that one of the largest areas for potential conflict is dealing with employees. Until very recently, the employer clearly held the upper hand—aside from unionized work forces, the employer could hire and fire at will. That is no longer true. Federal antidiscrimination laws governing race, sex, national origin, religion, and age considerably complicate the employer's life.

Even more recently, the age-old and hitherto sacrosanct doctrine of "at will termination" has come under heavy attack, and the fusillade may soon cause it to collapse altogether. Many responsible observers see this area as a fertile ground for employee-employer conflicts in the next several years.

The at-will doctrine holds that an employer may fire an employee without a contract for any reason whatsoever, or even for no reason. This doctrine is being challenged in state after state, and has begun to fall. Some states have carved out a "public policy" exception, so that employers may not legally fire someone carrying on an activity protected by the public policy of the state (for instance, cooperating with the police). Other states have read a "for cause only" policy into their employee laws. Still other states, such as New York, have said that certain actions or statements by the employer (for example, language in an employee handbook) may be interpreted as being an employment contract. The changing boundaries of this law make the employer's position increasingly difficult when disputes with employees arise.

A preventive program aimed at brushing away the legal tinder will review all corporate employment policies, both to ensure that they are not internally inconsistent (for example, that the employment handbook squares with the actual practices of the personnel department), and also that they are consistent not only with the law as it is now, but as it is likely to be in the near future. In an area undergoing such rapid change, however, even that may not be enough. That is why some companies have created the position of *ombudsman* (derived originally from the Scandinavian practice).

The ombudsman is a neutral fact-finder, and in all instances is either a high company official with considerable respect at the highest management levels or has a contract spelling out his or her authority to conduct the office. Authorized to investigate complaints by employees, the ombudsman is empowered to talk to anyone in the company to uncover the facts and to make a recommendation to senior management about how to dispose of the case. Although most are salaried by the company, their duty is not to senior management, or even to employees, but to the facts. Good ombudsmen are true neutrals, and any abuse of this neutrality would cause them to forfeit all respect. Among the companies that have adopted an ombudsman program to deal with employee disputes are Control Data, Federal Express, IBM, McDonald's Corporation, American Optical Company, and the Bank of America.

Just how seriously some companies take this concept can be seen from the ombudsman program at McDonald's Corporation. From 1974 through 1984, the McDonald's ombudsman, a senior vice-president named John Cooke, handled more than 1,500 cases arising from complaints of both employees and franchisees. In only two instances has McDonald's CEO ever overturned his recommendation. As a result of the program, according to Cooke, the cases are getting far harder to resolve. That is a sign of success, not failure. It illustrates how a neutral fact-finder over the long haul can change an entire corporate culture. Years ago, managers made "gross mistakes," which the ombudsman could easily spot and demonstrate to management. Over the years, however, company employees have learned from their previous mistakes and are no longer making the obvious ones. Disputes in the mid-1980s are "down to the fine points."

Cooke hears some 45 franchisee cases a year, and between 150 and 180 employee complaints. The cases have quite a range: from personality conflicts between employees to disputes among fellow franchisees.

The byword of the ombudsman program is informality. Anyone can call, Cooke says, and no one is obligated to get clearance in advance from anyone in the company. Cooke has one full-time associate, and they spend considerable time on the telephone giving advice. When a full-scale inquiry is demanded (one in which Cooke will travel to the operator's or employer's site), the regional manager or employee's supervisor must first be notified.

When a licensee requests a full-scale investigation, another operator from the outside is called in and travels with Cooke to the trouble spot. The outside operator is not reimbursed for the time, and many even refuse to accept reimbursement for expenses. (Cooke investigates employee disputes on his own.)

Cooke speaks first to the aggrieved party. Once the complainant has had his say, Cooke will talk to the regional manager or supervisor. There is no sworn testimony; loose rules of evidence prevail. "This is not a debating society," Cooke says; "it's a fact-finding inquiry."

Following the interview with the complainant, the ombudsman and accompanying licensee interview the regional manager (or supervisor or other related parties). After those statements are taken, Cooke reviews the records and files, looking for information that might support the position of the aggrieved person.

When he has sifted through the statements and files, Cooke prepares a statement of findings, conclusions, and recommendations. This report is preliminary, and is circulated to the interested parties to permit them to catch any errors that have crept into the summary of the record. At this point the aggrieved party, the regional manager, or the supervisor may respond and take issue with the conclusions and recommendations.

The report is then submitted to management, which has one week to consider the ombudsman's recommendations. If the ombudsman upholds a licensee's complaint, the regional manager may accept the recommendation, thus ending the matter. If the regional manager rejects the recommendation, Cooke may appeal to the zone manager, a higher-level executive. If the zone manager also rejects the report, Cooke may then appeal to the company president.

Likewise, when the ombudsman rejects the complainant's position, the aggrieved party may appeal up the chain to the president, and in that event the ombudsman, showing his impartiality, actually helps the aggrieved party prepare the appeal. About 10 to 15 percent of the cases are appealed to the president each year.

Cooke prefers to wrap up each case within two to three weeks. In practice, most cases take somewhat longer, probably averaging sixty days from the first phone call to the final resolution. Cooke says he is sustained by "one positive thing" that all seem to come away with, even if their positions were not upheld: "The ombudsman did his homework." That is the signal that the system is working. Because the program is entirely voluntary, operators or employers can always go to court, and some do. But many say, "I don't hate the company, I just want a hearing, and I'll accept your conclusion, even if I lose."

If all companies could install systems that instilled that belief in those who work for them, preventive law will have won the day.

13

IF YOU HAVE
TO GO TO COURT

No matter how hard you try to avoid it, your company will occasionally wind up in court. Your adversary may be unwilling to use an ADR mechanism, or the case may be one of those rare ones unsuitable to resolution except through adjudication. But being in court does not mean that the ADR repertoire is exhausted. New techniques have been developed in recent years to help speed the case and reduce its cost even in court.

Let the Judge Help You Settle

Most judges like cases to settle before trial, and many will join in or even engineer an effort to settle. Unfortunately, many judges think that a reasonable settlement can be arrived at by calling in the plaintiff's counsel and asking, "How much do you demand?," summoning the defendant's counsel and asking, "How much are you prepared to give?," and then, by an astute calculation, concluding that the case is worth some figure in the middle, usually the average of the two. That kind of process, repeated day in and day out in courts throughout the country, is inadequate. Indeed, knowing that a judge is likely to engage in it, the parties are likely to aggravate the dispute, each putting its dollar figure at the upper or lower extreme.

Some imaginative judges do better. And under a change in the federal court rules adopted in August 1983, federal judges now have the power to do much better. A few do, and their example may be widely imitated during the next few years among their colleagues and by state judges, many of whom have had similar powers for a long time.

The federal rules now permit the judge to hold a pretrial settlement conference and a pretrial discovery conference at the request of either party or at the judge's own behest *at a very early stage of the proceeding.* Among the topics discussed at the pretrial settlement conference are "the possibility of settlement or the use of extrajudicial procedures to resolve the dispute." At the discovery conference, the judge may lay down a strict order setting forth the time to be allowed for discovery and the issues to be covered.

The judge may direct the parties' attorneys to be present. Although the rule does not say that they may order it, some judges ask a business representative of the client to be present in court as well. If at first glance this seems a nuisance, the disruption of a busy schedule, think again. For an afternoon spent in court early in the case can save weeks or even months in court two or three years later.

This is so for many reasons. One exceedingly important reason is that here, just as in a minitrial, the client comes to see the lawyer performing on its behalf. A lawyer who knows that the client will be there is likely to prepare harder and in a different way than when he or she supposes the conference to be a perfunctory one in the presence only of the judge and the adversary counsel. The lawyer will want to be in control of the facts and the issues at an early stage, and will not want to seem to be saying to the judge that there is no possibility of settlement or that the pretrial discovery phase will consume two years or more.

Another reason is that the judge can get an immediate reaction to settlement proposals when the business representatives are present. Moreover, the business executives can even spark settlement proposals and can supply facts that will lead to settlement. Chicago Federal District Judge John F. Grady likes to tell the story of one suit in which the parties were about to embark on a series of depositions to establish whether one of the companies was doing business in Illinois as defined in the so-called long-arm statute. There had been considerable wrangling by the lawyers before the conference, and they went at it heatedly in front of Judge Grady. As it happened, he had asked the two chief executive officers to attend. They listened to the debate more and more incredulously, until one finally blurted out: "There isn't any question that we do business in Illinois." Potential months of discovery were thus eliminated.

Boston Federal District Judge Robert E. Keeton has given several other reasons for the importance of attendance by corporate representatives. These reasons all relate to the education of the executives, who will thereby see the case in a different light.

First, the executives will learn that they are not entitled to have their case tried on a priority basis. Many executives suppose that their case is so important the judge will surely find a way to get to it first. That simply is not so. They will learn that the case is likely to be two or three years away from trial, even if the lawyers are ready to proceed.

Second, the executives will learn that the litigation expenses they will incur by waiting and trying the case will be far greater than they had supposed. Of course, if the company had insisted on a litigation budget, the executives might not be surprised by what they learn; even so, the conference will serve as a useful check on the budgeting process.

Third, "in many intercorporate disputes that go through trial, total litigation costs exceed the difference between what would have been the parties' best estimates, as of the time of filing suit, of the expected outcome of the case, if they had bothered to make considered estimates." In other words, the executives may learn that taking the case through trial will cost each party more than it has believed it will make or save by doing so.

Fourth, pathological cases exist because the parties themselves do not have good information. Judge Keeton defines the *pathological case* as one in which disputing corporations "persist in either all-out adversary dispute resolution, reaching its consummation in trial and appeal, or—even more often— a ritual of bloodletting discovery in which they spend an amount equal to a very large fraction of the difference between considered best estimates of outcome before the two key decision-makers decide it's time to negotiate seriously." They do not refuse to negotiate because they are irrational, Judge Keeton says. Rather, they fail to negotiate because they are uninformed and distrustful of each other.

A pretrial conference with executives attending from both companies can overcome these difficulties. The business representatives will pick up facts galore, facts they may never have heard from their counsel. And they will meet each other face to face, a prospect that is highly unlikely outside the judge's chambers. Few lawyers will advise clients to meet face to face with their adversaries; lawyers prefer to bargain with other lawyers. Yet if the corporate decision-makers can meet in chambers, they can assess each other and can even meet by themselves (much in the style of a minitrial) immediately after to see whether the dispute can be sensibly resolved.

For all these reasons, a pretrial conference which corporate decision-makers attend should be the norm rather than the exception. That is especially so as judges become more sophisticated in the kinds of settlement talks they hold. One example of the lengths to which judges can and do go is the courtroom of Connecticut Senior Federal District Judge Robert C. Zampano. In a speech in late 1984 to the Westchester-Fairfield Corporate Counsel Association, Judge Zampano outlined the process that has resulted in high settlement rates of cases filed in his court.

First, he urges that settlement conferences be set as soon after filing as is convenient for the judge. In one case only three months old, with discovery barely underway, "the pleadings and preliminary moving papers stacked almost a foot high." At the conference, the lawyers said that they had already billed $200,000 in time related to discovery, which would extend at least another eight months to a year, and that trial would take at least a month of court time. But after "intense negotiations," the case was settled in two days.

Second, the parties themselves should be prepared to talk with the judge and not stand silent while the lawyers speak. Here is how Judge Zampano puts it:

> I usually first see and speak with plaintiff and his counsel privately. As a general rule, I chat with the plaintiff about his background and his prior experience with litigation. Sooner or later I will then ask the person just to sit back and "tell me about your case." Many times we engage in lively, interesting, and engaging colloquy with respect to the merits of the case. Sometimes I play the devil's advocate, other times I do not. The most important feature of the discussion is to give the person a full opportunity to be heard, in his or her own way. I try to put myself in the shoes of the party to understand exactly the source of the grievance and what type of settlement he or she believes would be just and fair. Generally, there is an open and frank discussion of attorney's fees, the availability of witnesses and documents to support the case, the inconvenience of a trial, and the rock bottom settlement terms, beyond which the individual will not give in one degree. This may come as a surprise, but generally counsel does not interject comments, but seems satisfied to have the client "talk the case over with the judge" with respect to the strengths and weaknesses of the case and the areas of reasonable and prudent settlement.

The same procedure is then followed with the defendant and defense counsel.

After these initial meetings, Judge Zampano may meet separately with the lawyers on another day, and still later with the management representatives individually "to review the issues, to discuss candidly the apparent strengths and weaknesses of the case from the attorney's point of view, to convert the legal issues as best I can into a businessman's language, and to fashion a fair and reasonable resolution which has appeal to them as corporate, business leaders." In doing so, Judge Zampano follows five guidelines:

1. The executives are told that the discussions are confidential.
2. The executives must have adequate time to talk to the judge, and the discussions usually last several hours.
3. The executives are encouraged to speak freely with each other, and even to meet by themselves without lawyers or the judge.
4. The final settlement must make financial, commercial, and business sense.
5. Neither side must come away from the settlement believing that it has lost.

When the judge plays a reasonable role in the pretrial settlement conference, especially when he extends himself as does Judge Zampano and several other federal judges who are actively interested in the psychology of settlement, most cases can be resolved short of trial. But some cases will not settle, even with judicial intervention of the sort just discussed. Then, other mechanisms can be brought into play.

One such mechanism, available in only a few courts now but likely to spread in the next few years, is pretrial court-mandated mediation. A significant pretrial mediation effort in the Chicago courts (Cook County) has been underway since 1982, and a similar program has been adopted in federal courts in Michigan. All civil cases coming to the courts are first submitted to mediation by a judge of the court, who is empowered to supervise all pretrial matters necessary to readying a case for trial.

If the case fails to settle after the mediation effort, the

case will go to trial before a different judge. A party may be liable to sanctions, however, if the ultimate verdict does not differ significantly—that is, by a certain percentage—from a settlement offer made by the other side prior to trial. (For example, a plaintiff who refuses a settlement offer of $100,000 and does not recover more than $110,000, 10 percent more than the offer, may be liable to pay the defendant's legal costs of trial.) Court-sponsored pretrial mediation efforts cannot be created privately, but private analogues are certainly possible, and we consider them next.

Let Someone Else Help You Settle

If the judge alone cannot bring the case to settlement, someone else might be able to do so. The rules of most courts permit the judge to appoint an individual to oversee the details of a case prior to trial. If legal issues arise, the judge must rule, but many intermediate decisions can be delegated to this *special master*. Conventionally, the special master sits to hear arguments over such issues as whether one party should have an extra week to produce certain documents. But the special master's role need not be so sharply limited. On the contrary, a special master can be used in two different ways to prompt settlements. One way is as a neutral advisor or mediator in a case involving two parties (or relatively few additional parties). The other way is as a management consultant to oversee the flow of a number of related cases.

Assume you have had a pretrial settlement conference, and although the judge has suggested a possible resolution, you or the other party reject it. You need not be resigned to facing trial. You might at that point ask for the remaining issues to be mediated, following the procedures outlined in Chapter 7. The mediator need not be a court-appointed master. But the mediator or neutral advisor (or panel of advisors) may be appointed by the court to assist with the settlement talks. This is most sensibly done when technical issues are involved and experts would be useful in listening to the arguments of both sides. Appointment of the neutral advisor or advisors will be done with the consent of both parties, just as they would mutually choose the neutral advisor in a minitrial.

Judge Zampano has developed a general plan for the employment of a panel of neutral experts in complex cases. Four guidelines apply, to which the parties must consent before the procedure can be used. First, the advisors may talk to all parties, privately and separately, or together, and may also talk to the lawyers and the expert witnesses scheduled to testify. Second, the parties pay equal amounts for the advisor's services, if the case settles. If the case does not settle, the loser pays the advisor's fee. Third, the advisor's recommendation for settlement is not binding. Fourth, if the case is not settled, the advisor may be called as a "court-appointed" expert witness and may submit his findings to the jury.

At the other extreme, special masters may be appointed as management experts to expedite the handling of dozens or hundreds of related cases. Two notable instances in which this process has been used are the seventy-odd consolidated asbestos personal injury lawsuits now in federal court in Cleveland and the thousand toxic waste personal injury cases now in federal court in Alabama. In each court, the judge has appointed a special master to develop a plan by which the cases can first be made ready for settlement discussions and then be processed expeditiously if some do not settle and must go to trial. In the Cleveland asbestos cases, the special masters (two were appointed) developed a means of valuing the worth of each case, based on an assessment of the experience in Cleveland with cases of similar characteristics. A separate case management plan requires unsettled cases to be presented to the court in clusters at specified intervals.

The key advantage of the special master is flexibility. The special master is not locked into any formula; he or she need follow no prescribed path. If your case seems unresolvable, even after discussions with the judge, you should talk to your lawyer about how the appointment of a special master—or reference to an outside mediator—can still bring about a mutually agreeable settlement.

Let Someone Help
You Manage Your Discovery

The special master—or a panel of neutrals—might usefully be employed to oversee the discovery process in cases that remain destined for litigation. Richard M. Rosenbleeth, a partner in the Philadelphia law firm of Blank Rome Comisky & McCauley, has suggested that a system of *alternative discovery dispute resolution (ADDR)* is the answer to one of the most baneful aspects of the whole litigation system—discovery disputes. He suggests that judges be called on to appoint a panel of senior judges and respected senior practicing attorneys to oversee the nagging problems that arise in complex discovery—when one party balks at turning material over, or delays, or makes unconscionable demands. As matters stand now, such disputes must be referred to the trial judge.

Most judges are understandably reluctant to involve themselves too deeply in the minutiae of the pretrial process. But a single discovery master or panel would not be subject to as many institutional restraints: It would have the time to learn the intricacies of the discovery issues and it could meet more easily with the parties and under more circumstances—for example, *during* a deposition, rather than days or weeks afterward. Moreover, since the litigants would be paying for the panelists' time, they would have marked incentives not to misuse or overuse their services.

Rosenbleeth sums up the advantages of ADDR:

The panelists could rule on disputes arising during discovery, ascertain the good faith compliance with court-imposed discovery orders, make preliminary rulings on privilege claims and other problems incidental to document production, preside at the taking of depositions, and rule on disputes relating to interrogatories.

In certain large cases, like the Agent Orange litigation and the Justice Department's antitrust prosecution of American Telephone & Telegraph, special masters were appointed for just such a purpose. There is no reason to believe that the system outlined here would not be useful in cases far smaller— and thus far more prevalent—than those.

Joint Defense

Increasingly today, corporations find themselves in good company in court: They are co-defendants with many other businesses in the same lawsuit. Plaintiff's lawyers have learned to sue not just one company, but all that could conceivably be made to pay: manufacturer, distributor, insurer, shipper, and others. All too often in the past, the co-defendants have wasted scarce dollars, time, and energy in fighting among themselves. Suspicious of everyone, each defendant fields a full team of litigators and treats each co-defendant in the same adversary manner as it treats the plaintiff(s). Such an approach can no longer be sustained. Today, co-defendants must learn to mount a *joint defense.*

But they can be brought to cooperate only if they see a way to resolve their mutual differences. After all, one co-defendant might be many times more culpable than the others—or so the others might believe.

The answer here is that many ADR techniques are available to aid co-defendants in resolving their own differences. Negotiation, mediation, and minitrials can make the defendants friends rather than antagonists. In perhaps the most potent use of these techniques, co-defendants in cases in which large damages are threatened can allocate the damages among themselves *very early on,* thus avoiding the divisiveness that destroys any defense. They can do this privately, and without conceding liability to the plaintiff. They can also negotiate the ways in which their defense teams will cooperate, dividing the workload instead of dividing themselves. One company's defense team might concentrate on the liability, another's on the issue of damages. However it is done, in these cases joint defense will prove not merely useful, but vital.

The Summary Jury Trial

Finally, an important innovation just beginning to spread throughout the federal court system, and easily adapted to the state courts, is the *summary jury trial*. It was the brainchild in the late 1970s of Cleveland Federal District Judge Thomas D. Lambros (the same judge who appointed the special management masters in the asbestos cases). In essence, it is a means of submitting a highly abbreviated trial to a mock jury composed of real jurors.

As the concept has spread from Ohio to courts in California, Colorado, Hawaii, Massachusetts, Montana, Michigan, Oklahoma, Pennsylvania, and elsewhere, the summary jury trial has picked up numerous variations. But in essence, it works as follows. The judge sets a firm summary jury trial date, usually only a few months after the case has been filed. The lawyers prepare for it as they would prepare for a minitrial. But the actual hearing is even shorter than that for a minitrial: The entire case may take place in a single morning or afternoon. The jury of six, culled from the regular jury pool, is empaneled. Its verdict is not binding, but the jurors do not know this until they have rendered it. They are told instead that a new procedure has been devised that will let the case be disposed of in half a day, and that after reaching their verdict they can go home.

In Cleveland, the lawyers alone are permitted to speak. In Michigan and other courts, the lawyers may put witnesses and their clients on the stand, as long as they stay within the time limits. The only substantive limitation is that only facts that would be admissible in a real trial may be presented at the summary jury trial. No cross-examination or objections by the other side are allowed. When the presentations are complete, the judge will instruct the jury in summary fashion—and in lay language—for about ten minutes. The jury then retires to reach its verdict. In some courts, the verdict must be unanimous; in others, a split verdict will do. The verdict is announced in open court to both sides.

Once the verdict is announced, the jury is fully informed about the nature of the process and told that the verdict is not binding. The jurors are encouraged, however, to stay in court and speak to the lawyers and the parties about how and why they deliberated. Because the parties—in the case of corporations, responsible executives—must attend the summary jury trial, they have an unparalleled opportunity to learn first hand how an actual jury saw the case. Immediately following the discussions with the jury, the parties and lawyers meet (either separately or with the judge) to hold settlement talks.

Settlement rates are high. In the Cleveland federal court, the summary jury trial process has led to settlements in more than 90 percent of the cases submitted to it; in other courts, the rate is well over 50 percent. The high rate stems from an informed understanding of the limits of each party's position and how it appears to a jury. It also stems from a psychological factor: Neither the lawyers nor the parties are especially willing to go through trial again. Notes Kalamazoo, Michigan, Federal District Judge Richard A. Enslen, who has sent some twenty cases through summary jury trials: "[The clients] came to the courtroom, they saw the psychological clash they had been waiting for, they were either relieved or upset with the jury verdict, and they were not too willing to go on and do this process again."

The lesson of these examples is plain. Even in court, there

are alternatives to trial, alternatives that are cheaper, quicker, and far less disruptive to the business. But each requires *active participation* by business executives with the lawyers in shaping and working through the process of dispute resolution.

14

WHERE CAN WE GO FROM HERE?

We have presented in short compass a panorama of the alternative dispute resolution mechanisms emerging across America during the past few years. As exciting as these developments may be (and we believe that many more are yet to come—from the practicing bar, from within the corporations, and from the courts), they are a long way from being even partly realized. Most of corporate America—lawyers and executives—is unfamiliar with the techniques now being pioneered. Many of the relatively few who do know about them remain skeptical. In order for ADR to achieve its maximum potential, much remains to be done.

A good deal of the task is for the technicians—the lawyers, judges, and managers who, in specific cases, will craft new processes and ingenious wrinkles on existing processes. We expect to see an explosive proliferation of ADR mechanisms throughout the second half of the 1980s. As these techniques emerge, the growing literature on dispute resolution will carry their story along.

But even the technical development depends to a great extent on the creation of a receptive climate throughout the United States. A useful tool is useless if the intended beneficiary refuses to put it to use. Accordingly, we believe that the American business manager must shoulder some of the burden in creating the climate in which alternative dispute resolution can flourish and grow. How can this be done?

We have already noted that one of the strengths of America is its richness in "people" resources. Tens of thousands of individuals across the country are able—and would be willing if given the opportunity—to play a constructive role in the resolution of individual disputes. Every corporation ought to nurture this potential source of dispute resolvers. Companies can do so by actively seeking to build networks of neutrals—neutral experts, neutral minitrial advisors, mediators, and the like. They can do so by speaking out publicly—from the CEO on down—for the need to search out alternative means of resolving disputes. And they can do so by announcing their own commitment to the processes of alternative dispute resolution. We believe that if corporations were publicly to commit to use ADR whenever reasonably suitable and available, rather than to seek litigious solutions to their problems, ADR would become a major force in American business and in all the means by which we seek to damp conflict in this country.

One development deserves special mention, because it may serve as an initial vehicle by which businesses can make that commitment. The development was the brainchild of Jay Topkis, a senior partner in the New York law firm of Paul Weiss Rifkind Wharton & Garrison. In June 1983, at the Center for Public Resources third annual meeting in Aspen, Colorado, Topkis suggested a Public Pledge. The idea was simple. A company should subscribe to a short written pledge to seek an alternative means of resolving a dispute with any company that signed the same pledge. The fact of signing should be made public. It would not only help foster ADR, Topkis mused, but would also be a potential public relations boon for the corporation.

Today Topkis's suggestion is a reality, formally known as the Corporate Policy Statement, but informally known as the ADR Pledge. Almost 100 major American corporations have, *through their CEOs*, officially adopted the language reprinted in Appendix F, and committed to the use of ADR with any company also signing the pledge. We emphasize that the pledge has been taken not by the companies' lawyers, but by their CEOs. (The list of the first ninety-six signatories is given in Appendix F.) That list is impressive because it shows that the times are ripe for ADR and that many of the top CEOs in the nation have understood immediately how important the concept is to them and their companies not merely in the long run, but right now.

Note that the pledge is not binding: It does not require any company to forsake any legal rights or to renounce going to court in any particular dispute. It simply sets forth as a moral imperative the company's willingness to explore settlement of a dispute through appropriate alternative means.

How might adoption of the pledge be broadened? Of course, any CEO reading this chapter is invited to sign it and announce that he or she has signed it, and any manager reading about the pledge is invited to call it to the attention of the CEO and senior management. We encourage any company that signs the pledge to report to the Center for Public Resources that it has done so. CPR maintains a registry that is updated periodically and publicly, so that all will know the names of signatory companies.

We believe that companies can promote an even more active commitment by circulating the language of the pledge to other companies with which they do business and, perhaps more important, by putting it on the agenda of the associations and trade groups to which they belong. A local Chamber of Commerce; a local, regional, or national trade association; and even an executives' luncheon club can be the vehicle through which awareness of the pledge and its broad potential can be spread. More, as discussion of the pledge becomes common, knowledge of ADR in general will be disseminated to ever-widening publics. And this last is the crucial point: With the knowledge that disputes *can* be resolved outside the court comes the *willingness* to do so. Only with that widespread willingness will ADR come of age.

We end as we began: The resolution of disputes is in your hands. Together with your lawyers, you can forge the means of ending costly and disruptive disputes and go on about your business.

APPENDIX A

CPR Model Minitrial Agreement for Business Disputes

As published May 7, 1985

PURPOSES

The informal procedure known as a minitrial, consisting of an adversarial "information exchange," followed by management negotiations, has become a highly successful form of business dispute resolution. Set forth below is a model agreement for a minitrial to resolve a business dispute.

The success of minitrials has been due in large part to the voluntary nature and flexibility of the process and to the cooperation, flexibility and creativity of disputants' counsel in developing procedures best suited for their particular situations. The Center for Public Resources (CPR) encourages parties to modify this model agreement, or to draw up their own agreement, which, for example, may provide for a minitrial with or without a Neutral Advisor or may alter the role of the Neutral Advisor.

The minitrial can be used in a variety of circumstances. Parties to an existing dispute can use this model agreement, whether or not the dispute is in litigation. The model agreement can be adopted for disputes between U.S. companies; for disputes involving foreign companies; and, with minor modifications, for disputes between a government entity and a private company. The model agreement should facilitate the drafting of commercial agreement clauses providing for dispute resolution by minitrial, by enabling the draftsman to incorporate the model agreement by reference.

The model agreement is not self-executing, but is to be invoked through execution of an "initiating agreement," as described below. A party may withdraw from the process at any time before its conclusion.

A sample schedule and a commentary follow the model agreement. The schedule is illustrative of the time typically required for the various phases of the proceeding.

CPR has established the CPR Judicial Panel, consisting of eminent former judges, legal academics and other leaders of the bar who may assist in structuring a minitrial and may serve as Neutral Advisor in a minitrial. In conjunction with its Judicial Panel services, CPR is available, at the request of a party to a business dispute, to interest the other party or parties in entering into a minitrial. A brochure listing the members of the Judicial Panel and describing services they may perform is available.

CPR has considerable expertise in the conduct of minitrials and has produced a Minitrial Workbook, which includes case histories and relevant forms. CPR also has a clearinghouse of information and literature on alternative dispute resolution.

MODEL AGREEMENT

1. Institution of Minitrial Proceeding

1.1. Parties to a dispute may commence a minitrial proceeding by entering into a written agreement (the "initiating agreement") to conduct a minitrial. The initiating agreement shall describe the matter in dispute and shall state either that the parties agree to follow this model agreement, as modified by the initiating agreement, or that the parties agree to other procedures set forth or identified in the initiating agreement. A copy of the initiating agreement should be filed with the Center for Public Resources, 680 Fifth Avenue, New York, New York 10019.

1.2. Various time periods referred to in this model agreement are measured from the date of the initiating agreement, which hereafter is called the Commencement Date.

2. Minitrial Panel

2.1. The minitrial panel shall consist of a Neutral Advisor and one member of management from each party. Each such member shall have appropriate authority to negotiate a settlement on behalf of the party he or she represents.

2.2. The parties shall attempt to select a Neutral Advisor who is mutually acceptable to them, and who may be, but need not be, a member of the CPR Judicial Panel. The functions of the Neutral Advisor are those stated in this agreement.

2.3. If the parties have not agreed on a Neutral Advisor within fifteen days from the Commencement Date, any party may request CPR to nominate candidates. Within ten days of receiving such a request, CPR shall submit to the parties the names of not fewer than five nominees, together with a brief statement of each nominee's qualifications and the per diem or hourly rates charged by such nominee. Each party may strike from the list the names of all persons who are unacceptable to it and number the remaining names to indicate an order of preference. Each party shall mail the list to CPR within seven days of having received it. CPR will designate the Neutral Advisor from the panel members acceptable to all parties, in accordance with the designated order of mutual preference. If a party does not return the list of nominees within seven days, CPR will assume that all of the nominees are acceptable to that party. If no nominee is acceptable to all parties, CPR will schedule a meeting with the parties to agree on a Neutral Advisor.

2.4. Each party shall promptly disclose to the other party or parties any circumstances known to it which would cause reasonable doubt regarding the impartiality of an individual under consideration or appointed as a Neutral Advisor. Any such individual shall promptly disclose any such circumstances to the parties. If any such circumstances have been disclosed, the individual shall not serve as Neutral Advisor, unless all parties agree.

2.5. Prior to the minitrial information exchange described in Section 6 hereof, and unless all parties otherwise agree, no party, nor anyone acting on its behalf, shall unilaterally communicate with the Neutral Advisor, except as specifically provided for herein.

2.6. The parties will jointly and promptly send to the Neutral Advisor such materials as they may agree upon for the purpose of familiarizing him or her with the facts and issues in the dispute.

2.7. The parties may jointly seek the advice and assistance of the Neutral Advisor or of CPR in interpreting this agreement and on procedural matters. The parties shall comply promptly with all reasonable requests by the Neutral Advisor for documents or other information relevant to the dispute.

2.8. The Neutral Advisor's per diem or hourly charge will be established at the time of his or her appointment. Unless the parties otherwise agree, (a) the fees and expenses of the Neutral Advisor, as well as any other expenses of the minitrial, will be borne equally by the parties; and (b) each party shall bear its own costs of the proceedings.

2.9. On or before thirty days from the Commencement Date, by written notice to each other party and the Neutral Advisor, each party shall select a member of its management to serve on the Panel. If a party later desires to designate a different member of management, it shall promptly notify each other party and the Neutral Advisor of the substitution.

3. Court Proceedings

3.1. If on the Commencement Date no litigation is pending between the parties with respect to the subject matter of the minitrial, no party shall commence such litigation until the minitrial proceedings have terminated in accordance with Section 9 hereof. Execution of the initiating agreement shall toll all applicable statutes of limitation until the minitrial proceedings have terminated. The parties will take such other action, if any, required to effectuate such tolling.

3.2. If on the Commencement Date litigation is pending between the parties with respect to the subject matter of the minitrial, the parties will promptly (a) present a joint motion to the Court to request a stay of all proceedings pending conclusion of the minitrial proceedings; and (b) request the Court to enter an order protecting the confidentiality of the minitrial and barring any collateral use by the parties of any aspect of the minitrial in any pending or future litigation; provided, however, that the grant of such stay and protective order shall not be a condition to the continuation of the minitrial proceeding.

4. Discovery

4.1. If one or more of the parties have a substantial need for discovery in order to prepare for the minitrial information exchange, the parties shall attempt in good faith to agree on a minimum plan for strictly necessary, expeditious discovery. Should they fail to reach agreement, any party may request a joint meeting with the Neutral Advisor to explain points of agreement and disagreement. The Neutral Advisor shall promptly make a recommendation as to the scope of discovery and time allowed therefor.

4.2. Should the minitrial not result in a settlement of the dispute, discovery taken in preparation for the minitrial information exchange may be used in any pending or future judicial proceeding between the parties relating to the dispute. Such discovery shall not restrict a party's ability to take additional discovery at a later date in any such proceeding, including additional depositions from persons deposed.

5. Briefs and Exhibits

5.1. Before the minitrial information exchange, the parties shall exchange, and submit to the Neutral Advisor, briefs, as well as all documents or other exhibits on which the parties intend to rely during the minitrial information exchange. The parties shall agree upon the length of such briefs, and on the date on which such briefs, documents and other exhibits are to be exchanged.

6. Conduct of Minitrial Information Exchange

6.1. The minitrial information exchange shall be held before the minitrial panel at a place agreed to by the parties, on a date agreed to by the parties and the Neutral Advisor.

6.2. During the information exchange each party shall make a presentation of its best case, and each party shall be entitled to a rebuttal. The order and permissible length of presentations and rebuttals shall be determined by agreement between the parties.

6.3. The presentations and rebuttals of each party may be made in any form, and by any individuals, as desired by such party. Presentations by fact witnessess and expert witnesses shall be permitted.

6.4. No rules of evidence, including rules of relevance, will apply at the information exchange, except that the rules pertaining to privileged communications and attorney work product will apply.

6.5. The Neutral Advisor will moderate the information exchange.

6.6. Presentations may not be interrupted, except that during each party's presentation, and following such presentation, any member of the Panel may ask clarifying questions of counsel or other persons appearing on that party's behalf. No member of the panel may limit the scope or substance of a party's presentation. Each party may ask questions of opposing counsel and witnesses during scheduled open question-and-answer exchanges, and during that party's rebuttal time if the parties so agree.

6.7. The information exchange shall not be recorded by any means. However, subject to Section 8, persons attending the information exchange may take notes of the proceedings.

6.8. In addition to counsel, each management representative may have advisors in attendance at the information exchange, provided that each other party and the Neutral Advisor shall have been notified of the identity of such advisors at least ten days before commencement of the information exchange.

7. Negotiations Between Management Representatives

7.1. At the conclusion of the information exchange, the management representatives shall meet, by themselves, and shall attempt to agree on a resolution of the dispute. By agreement, other members of their teams may be invited to participate in the meetings.

7.2. At the request of any management representative, the Neutral Advisor will render an oral opinion as to the likely outcome at trial of each issue raised during the information exchange. Following that opinion, the management representatives will again attempt to resolve the dispute. If all management representatives agree to request a written opinion on such matters, the Neutral Advisor shall render such a written opinion within fourteen days. Following issuance of any such written opinion, the management representatives will again attempt to resolve the dispute.

8. Confidentiality

8.1. The entire process is a compromise negotiation. All offers, promises, conduct and statements, whether oral or written, made in the course of the minitrial proceeding by any of the parties, their agents, employees, experts and attorneys, and by the Neutral Advisor, who is the parties' joint counsel (or agent if not an attorney) for the purpose of these compromise negotiations, are confidential. Such offers, promises, conduct and statements are subject to FRE 408 and are inadmissible and not discoverable for any purpose, including impeachment, in litigation between the parties to the minitrial or other litigation. However, evidence that is otherwise admissible or discoverable shall not be rendered inadmissible or nondiscoverable as a result of its presentation or use at the minitrial.

8.2. The Neutral Advisor will be disqualified as a trial witness, consultant, or expert for any party, and his or her oral and written opinions will be inadmissible for all purposes in this or any other dispute involving the parties hereto.

Termination of Proceedings

9.1. The minitrial proceedings shall be deemed terminated if and when (a) the parties have not executed a written settlement of their dispute on or before the forty-fifth day following conclusion of the minitrial information exchange (which deadline may be extended by mutual agreement of the parties), or (b) any party serves on each other party and on the Neutral Advisor a notice of withdrawal from the minitrial proceedings.

SAMPLE MINITRIAL SCHEDULE

Before the Minitrial Information Exchange

Commencement Date (CD): Parties sign filing agreement and file same with CPR (para. 1.1.).

CD + 10: Parties agree on Neutral Advisor (NA) (para. 2.2.).

CD + 10: If litigation is pending, parties' attorneys move to stay proceedings (para. 3.2.).

CD + 15: Parties' attorneys agree on discovery plan, including a sixty-day discovery schedule (para. 4.1.).

CD + 20: Parties' attorneys send material on dispute to NA (para. 2.6.).

CD + 30: Parties' attorneys agree on place and date for minitrial and on length of presentations, rebuttals, and responses (para. 6.1.–6.2.).

CD + 30: Parties determine form of briefs and date for submission of briefs and exhibits (para. 5.1.).

CD + 30: Parties give notice of selection of management members of panel (para. 2.9.).

CD + 75: Discovery is completed.

CD + 90: Parties exchange briefs and exhibits (para. 5.1.).

CD + 95: Parties give notice of advisors who will attend information exchange (para. 6.8.).

CD + 105: Information Exchange begins (para. 6.2.).

At the Minitrial Information Exchange

Day 1: 9:00–12:00 Plaintiff's case-in-chief
1:00– 2:00 Defendant's rebuttal
2:00– 3:00 Open question and answer exchange

Day 2: 9:00–12:00 Defendant's case-in-chief
1:00– 2:00 Plaintiff's rebuttal
2:00– 3:00 Open question-and-answer exchange

After the Minitrial Information Exchange

Day 2:   3:00–5:00 Negotiations
Day 3–21:   Reserved for negotiations (para. 7.1.).
Day 17:   NA submits written opinion, if requested (para. 7.2.).

CPR COMMENTARY ON MODEL MINITRIAL AGREEMENT

Counsel drafting a commercial agreement may incorporate the model minitrial agreement by reference. The following language is suggested:

> The parties intend that they will attempt in good faith to resolve any controversy or claim arising out of or relating to this agreement by a minitrial in accordance with the CPR Model Minitrial Agreement.

CPR does not consider the above clause as creating an enforceable right or obligation. The model agreement is not designed to be self-executing. CPR considers it an essential characteristic of the minitrial that it be entered into voluntarily by parties which wish to resolve a dispute in a private, rapid, cost-effective manner through an informal, collaborative process which will enable them to fashion their own solution. A minitrial is not likely to succeed without the genuine motivation of the parties to make it succeed.

Between reputable companies even an unenforceable statement of intent should carry considerable weight, and if a dispute should arise, such a statement would substantially increase the likelihood that the parties would make a serious effort to arrive at a compromise through the minitrial process, rather than seeking an adjudicative solution.

The commercial agreement also could provide that if a dispute arises, negotiations between executives would be the first step in attempting resolution; a minitrial the second step, if such negotiations should not succeed.

The role of CPR in the procedure is very limited. CPR believes that the minitrial should be a truly private process which succeeds through cooperation between the parties and between counsel.

CPR may make reasonable time charges for such services as it is asked to perform.

The paragraph numbers below refer to paragraphs in the model agreement:

1.1. CPR will not charge a fee for filing of the initiating agreement.

2.1. The model agreement provides for the appointment of a Neutral Advisor. CPR believes that a highly qualified Neutral Advisor can substantially enhance the prospects for success; however, successful minitrials also have been held without a Neutral Advisor. The parties have the option of dispensing with a Neutral Advisor.

2.2. In order for the Neutral Advisor's views to carry weight, the Neutral Advisor must be a person in whose impartiality and judgment all parties have full confidence. It is preferable that the Neutral Advisor be selected by mutual agreement, rather than through the nomination procedure set forth in paragraph 2.3.

2.9. The negotiations following the information exchange are more likely to succeed if the negotiators are objective and do not feel a need to defend past actions. It is preferable that the management representatives shall not have participated directly or actively in the events underlying the dispute. As a rule, the more senior the management representatives, the greater the range of options for a constructive solution they will perceive.

4.1. Discovery should be limited to that for which each party has a substantial need for purposes of the minitrial information exchange. As a rule, such discovery would be far less extensive than discovery conducted in preparation for a trial. The objective is to enable the parties, through limited discovery on the merits, in a short period to define the issues and to learn the principal strengths and weaknesses of their cases. If litigation between the parties is pending, any prior discovery in that litigation should be taken into account in determining the need for additional discovery.

6.2. The tone of the minitrial should be one of business-like problem solving. Nevertheless, counsel are expected to vigorously advocate their positions during the minitrial information exchange.

7.1. In some circumstances negotiations will be more productive if more than one representative of each party participates.

7.2. The Neutral Advisor also may assist in bringing about a settlement by mediating the negotiations. The initiating agreement may provide that the Neutral Advisor will serve as a mediator, or the management representatives may call on him to play that role during the negotiations.

APPENDIX B

Dispute Resolution Contract Clauses

The following two sets of provisions are for use in contracts in order to assure that future disputes arising out of the contracts will be submitted first to an ADR procedure. Clause 1 provides for a good-faith submission of the dispute to appropriate executives for direct negotiations about the subject in controversy. If those fail, the provision calls for negotiations on a procedure, such as a minitrial, to resolve the dispute without going to litigation. In its present form, the contract clause calls for the good faith of each party; it is nonbinding and may be canceled by its terms at any time.

Clause 2 is for use in a typical international joint venture. It provides for negotiation and a minitrial during a cooling-off period, during which all litigation is to be stayed.

CLAUSE 1

1. If a dispute arises under this Agreement which cannot be resolved by the personnel directly involved, either party may invoke this Dispute Resolution Procedure by giving written notice to the other designating an executive officer with appropriate authority to be its representative in negotiations relating to the dispute.

2. Upon receipt of this notice, the other party shall, within five business days, designate an executive officer with similar authority to be its representative.

3. The designated executive officers shall, following whatever investigation each deems appropriate, promptly enter into discussions concerning the dispute.

4. If the dispute is not resolved as a result of such discussions, either party may request the commencement of good faith negotiations with respect to a procedure for dealing with the dispute through means other than litigation.

5. Upon such request, counsel for the parties shall promptly communicate concerning the following and other related subjects:

 a. The mode of further proceeding (for example, a formal, nonbinding minitrial before a panel composed of executive officers of each of the parties, with or without an independent neutral chairman or advisor);

 b. A procedure and schedule for exchange of documents and other information related to the dispute;

 c. Ground rules and a schedule for the conduct of the selected mode of proceeding;

 d. Selection and compensation of the neutral chairman or advisor (if any).

6. Following the conclusion of any agreed upon formal procedure and receipt of the input of the neutral chairman or advisor (if any), the parties shall continue direct contacts at the executive management level and continue to attempt to resolve the dispute.

7. Either party may terminate the Dispute Resolution Procedure at any time and may thereafter pursue other available remedies.

CLAUSE 2

Except for any of the matters which require a unanimous vote at a properly constituted meeting of the Board of Directors, in the event of any dispute or disagreement among the Parties as to any provision of this Agreement (including any provision of any Schedule, Exhibit, or Related Agreement) and, without limiting the generality of the foregoing, any dispute relating to termination of the Joint Venture due to a prolonged and significant failure of the Joint Venture to perform according to the Business Plan, upon the written request of any Party, the matter shall immediately be referred jointly to the respective top managements of each party for decision. If such executives do not agree upon a decision within thirty (30) days after reference of the matter to them, any Party may within thirty (30) days, after the thirty (30) days' first reference, above, elect to utilize a nonbinding resolution procedure whereby each Party presents its case at a hearing before a panel consisting of a senior executive of each Party and a mutually acceptable judicial personage. . . . The Parties may be represented at the hearing by lawyers. Prior to the hearing the Parties shall meet to mutually agree on a set of ground rules for the hearing and a site therefore. In the event the Parties cannot reasonably and promptly agree on the ground rules, judicial personage, or hearing site, or any of the foregoing, if the Party initiating this dispute resolution procedure is X (Japanese company), the United States Consul

General in Tokyo, or whatever official is then exercising the powers and authority of such Consul General, shall designate the ground rules, judicial personage, or site, and, if the party initiating the dispute resolution procedure is Y (U.S. Company), the Japanese Consul General in Los Angeles, or whatever official is then exercising the powers and authority of such Consul General, shall designate the ground rules, judicial personage, or site. At the conclusion of the hearing, the senior executives of X and Y shall meet and attempt to resolve the matter. If the matter cannot be resolved at such meeting, the judicial personage may be called upon to render his opinion as to how the matter would be resolved had the hearing been a trial in a court of law. After the opinion is received, the senior executives shall meet and try again to resolve the matter. If the matter cannot be resolved at such meeting, then (X) may give the other Party notice of its intention to litigate. No litigation may commence concerning the matter in dispute until sixty (60) days have elapsed from the sending of the notice of intention to litigate. The Parties shall bear their respective costs incurred in connection with this procedure, except that the Parties shall share, in proportion to their ownership interests in the Joint Venture, the fees and expenses of the judicial personage, the costs of the facility for the hearing, and the fee or charge, if any, of the applicable Consul General.

APPENDIX C

Arbitration Clause

The following clause is the language typically used in contracts in which the parties agree to arbitrate any future disputes arising out of the contract according to the rules of the American Arbitration Association.

Any controversy or claim arising out of or relating to this contract, or the breach thereof, shall be settled by arbitration in accordance with the Commercial Arbitration Rules of the American Arbitration Association, and judgment upon the award rendered may be entered in any court having jurisdiction thereof.

APPENDIX D

The IBM–Hitachi Arbitration Procedure

In October 1983, the International Business Machines Corporation and Hitachi, Ltd., settled a year-long civil suit concerning Hitachi's alleged theft of IBM trade secrets. The resolution called for the establishment of a special three-person arbitration panel with jurisdiction to hear allegations of trade secret misuse and to award injunctions and compensatory and punitive damages. Because this panel has been widely hailed as a mechanism that could set an industry standard, the relevant portions of that agreement are set forth in this Appendix as an example of a private arbitration procedure that can be tailored to the disputants' needs.

In the event that any dispute, controversy or claim arises out of this Stipulation, Order and Judgment, including without limitation any dispute, controversy or claim relating to any alleged breach or violation thereof by a party, or the scope, interpretation, validity or termination thereof, the parties shall promptly refer the matter to the responsible executives of the parties who have been designated pursuant to paragraph 11(a) hereof for consideration and solution. Either party may commence such proceedings by delivering to the other party a written request for such a meeting. Unless otherwise agreed by the parties, the meeting shall commence in the United States within fourteen (14) days of receipt of such notice. Unless otherwise agreed by the parties, in the event that the parties are unable to resolve the matter between them within fourteen (14) days following the first meeting of the designated executives, either party may initiate proceedings for a final and binding resolution of such dispute, controversy or claim by arbitration in accordance with the procedures hereinafter set forth.

    (a) The arbitration shall be heard and determined by a panel of three persons. Each party shall have the right to designate one member of the panel, who shall be a responsible executive of that party. IBM hereby designates John E. Bertram as a member of the panel. Hitachi hereby designates Takeo Miura as a member of panel. The parties, prior to November 4, 1983, will designate a third member as Chairman of the panel (the 'Chairman'). The Chairman shall receive an annual retainer of at least thirty thousand dollars ($30,000) and shall agree to serve in any proceeding conducted pursuant to this Stipulation, Order and Judgment. The cost of the Chairman's annual retainer shall be shared equally by the parties. In addition, the Chairman shall be paid an hourly rate of at least one hundred fifty dollars ($150) plus all out-of-pocket expenses incurred in respect of any proceeding, which payments shall in the first instance be shared equally by the parties. All payments to the Chairman in respect of any proceeding shall be treated as costs of that proceeding and shall be apportioned at the close thereof as provided in paragraph 11(i).

(b) If either party's designated member of the panel resigns, dies or is otherwise incapacitated from serving or refuses to serve, that party shall promptly designate a replacement for such person. The failure of a party to designate a replacement for its designated member shall not disable the panel from hearing and determining any controversy that is otherwise properly before it, but the panel shall take no action for a period of fourteen (14) days following the commencement of such a vacancy, to permit the party to appoint a replacement. If the Chairman of the panel resigns, dies or is otherwise incapacitated from serving or refuses to serve, the parties shall confer promptly to agree upon a replacement. If the parties are unable to agree upon a replacement within thirty (30) days following his resignation, death, incapacitation or refusal to serve, this Court shall appoint such replacement. If any member of the panel was at the time of his resignation, death or incapacitation acting in respect of an ongoing arbitration, the replacement shall be empowered to act upon any record previously generated in such arbitration and in any further proceedings therein as if he had acted in respect of such proceeding from the commencement thereof.

(c) Decisions of the panel shall be made by majority vote. The panel is empowered to render awards enjoining a party from performing any act prohibited or compelling a party to perform any act directed by this Stipulation, Order and Judgment. Where the panel has determined that Hitachi has used, relied upon or benefited from Protected Information in any way in connection with any EDP Product, the panel shall enjoin the manufacture and marketing of such product, unless the panel expressly determines that such an injunction will inflict damage upon Hitachi which is grossly and excessively disproportionate to the value or significance of such Protected Information. In the case of Protected Information which has become Public Information prior to the date of the award, the duration of the injunction shall be for the period required lawfully to reverse engineer the product from the Public Information so disclosed.

In the case of Protected Information which has not become Public Information as of the date of the award, the duration of the injunction shall be the sum of: (1) the period until the Protected Information becomes Public Information and (2) the period required lawfully to reverse engineer the product from the Public Information so disclosed. In addition, the panel is empowered to award actual and punitive damages for any breach of this Stipulation, Order and Judgment. Where such damages are awarded for use of Protected Information by Hitachi, the measure of actual damages shall be the sum of (1) three times the value of the Protected Information used by Hitachi (such value being the greater of (a) the fully allocated cost to IBM of developing the Protected Information or (b) IBM's lost profits. In the event that the panel determines that any employee of IBM has willfully misused for IBM's benefit Hitachi's confidential material provided to IBM pursuant to paragraph 8 and that any corrective action taken by IBM is unsatisfactory, the panel may grant appropriate relief.

(d) The panel may issue such interim orders in accord with principles of equity as may be necessary to protect any party from irreparable harm during the pendency of any arbitration before it, including without limitation any order enjoining the manufacture or marketing of any Hitachi EDP Product anywhere in the world. Any such order shall be without prejudice to the final determination of the controversy.

(e) The proceeding before the panel shall be held where convenient for the Chairman at a location in the United States.

(f) The arbitration shall be conducted on an expedited schedule. Unless otherwise agreed by the parties, they shall make their initial submissions to the panel and the hearing shall commence within thirty (30) days of the initiation of proceedings. The hearing shall be completed within thirty (30) days thereafter.

(g) The award shall be made promptly by the panel, and, unless agreed by the parties, no later than thirty (30) days from the closing of the hearing. Any failure to render the award within the foregoing time period shall not affect the validity of such award. ·

(h) The arbitration shall be conducted in English. The initiating party shall make the necessary arrangements for the taking of a stenographic record. Each party shall make any necessary arrangements for the services of any interpreter required in respect of its witnesses and exhibits and shall bear the cost of such services. All documentation submitted to the panel will be in English unless the panel provides for submissions in Japanese in order to expedite the proceedings.

(i) The losing party shall pay all costs of the arbitration, including without limitation the cost of any stenographic record and the cost of any expert assistance retained pursuant to paragraph 11 (n) hereof, and all costs of any related inspection conducted pursuant to paragraph 8 hereof. In addition, the panel shall award to the prevailing party its reasonable attorneys' fees.

(j) The parties shall be entitled to discover all documents and information reasonably necessary for a full understanding of any legitimate issue raised in the arbitration. The parties may use all methods of discovery available under the Federal Rules of Civil Procedure, including but not limited to depositions, requests for admission and requests for production of documents. The time periods applied to these discovery methods shall be set by the panel so as to permit compliance with the scheduling provisions of paragraphs 11 (f) and (g) hereof.

(k) All papers, documents, or evidence, whether written or oral, filed with or presented to the panel shall be deemed by the parties and by the panel to be confidential information. No party or member of the panel shall disclose in whole or in part to any other Person any confidential information submitted in connection with the proceedings, except to the extent reasonably necessary to assist counsel in the proceeding or in preparation for the proceeding. Confidential information may be disclosed to the parties and their counsel and to qualified outside experts requested by counsel or retained by the panel to furnish technical or expert services or to give testimony at the proceeding. Outside experts shall be qualified by agreement of the parties or by order of the panel in the following manner: (1) before disclosure of confidential information is made to a proposed outside expert, his identity shall be given to the party by whom or on whose behalf the confidential information may be disclosed together with his address and a brief description of his professional and employment background and qualifications; (2) the party originally furnishing the confidential information or on whose behalf it was originally furnished, shall, prior to the disclosure, be entitled to object to such disclosure on the grounds that it can reasonably be expected that the disclosure will not remain confidential in accordance with this provision; (3) such objection shall be served within seven (7) days after receipt of notice, shall be stated in reasonable detail, and shall be in writing; (4) if the parties are unable to agree as to the merits of the objection within seven (7) days after its receipt, the matter shall be submitted to the panel; (5) before an outside expert shall be qualified, he shall deliver to counsel for the party originally furnishing the confidential information or on whose behalf it was originally furnished a legally binding written statement that he is fully familiar with the terms of this paragraph 11 (k), that he agrees to comply with the confidentiality terms of this paragraph 11 (k) and that he will not use any confidential information disclosed to him for personal or business advantage; and (6) no party, witness or member of the panel shall have any obligation of confidentiality pursuant to this paragraph 11 (k) with respect to any information which is in or becomes a part of the public domain through no fault of such party, witness or panel member.

(1) The decision or award rendered or made in connection with the arbitration shall be final and binding upon the parties thereto. The prevailing party may present the decision or award to this Court for confirmation pursuant to the provisions of the Federal Arbitration Act, 9 U.S.C. §§1-14, and this Court shall enter forthwith an order confirming such decision or award.

(m) Hitachi hereby submits to jurisdiction in any location chosen pursuant to paragraph 11 (e), for the purpose of conduct of any arbitration, and to the jurisdiction of this Court in connection with any action to compel arbitration pursuant to this Stipulation, Order and Judgment, for entry of judgment upon any decision or award rendered or made in connection with any proceeding conducted pursuant to this Stipulation, Order and Judgment, or for enforcement of such judgment, and agrees that it shall not assert or argue that this Court is an inconvenient forum for such action or proceeding or otherwise challenge the jurisdiction of or venue in this Court.

(n) The panel shall have the authority to retain such impartial expert assistance as it deems necessary to assist it in making a full and fair evaluation of the claims of the parties, to compensate any retained expert at an appropriate rate, and to reimburse any retained expert for all out-of-pocket expenses incurred in connection with any controversy.

(o) The arbitration shall be governed by such of the Commercial Arbitration Rules of the American Arbitration Association as are specified on Exhibit D hereto, except insofar as such specified rules are inconsistent with the provisions of this Stipulation, Order and Judgment.

APPENDIX E

A Sample Litigation Budget

BACKGROUND MEMORANDUM TO PRELIMINARY BUDGET FOR [ABC CORP.] v. [XYZ CORP.]

I. Nature of Representation

We have been asked to represent [XYZ Corporation] in a case filed against them by the [ABC Corporation] in the United States District Court, Southern District of New York. The complaint alleges various violations of federal and state antitrust laws, as well as of state franchise law, arising out of the termination of [ABC] as an [XYZ] distributor and seeks injunctive relief and damages.

II. Basic Assumptions

[XYZ] believes that this case is important to preserve the integrity of its distribution system and desires to defend this case fully. The annual proposed budget is obviously a preliminary estimate and will be reviewed periodically. As the case progresses and we can better judge [ABC's] litigation intentions and strategies, the budget will be revised as required in consultation with the client.

III. Basic Staffing

[A partner] will be responsible for managing and litigating the case and it is anticipated that he will devote a substantial portion of his time to the case. In addition, [a similar partner] will spend a limited amount of time on the case providing overall advice and counsel. There will be three associates assigned part-time to the case, perhaps one more if the volume of documents demands.

[Name] _____, a senior litigation associate, will be expected to spend up to 25% of his time on this case. He will assist [the partner] in all aspects of the case and take a major role in the discovery and pretrial phases.

[Name] _____, a senior antitrust associate, will spend approximately 15% of his time on the case. He will be principally responsible for the antitrust aspects of the case and will participate to the extent necessary and desirable in the overall litigation of the case.

[Name] _____, a junior litigation associate, will spend considerable time on this case and will become completely familiar with the facts and be principally responsible for coordinating the review of documents. There will be one paralegal assigned to this case.

The assumed billing rates are as follows (changes would, of course, increase the estimated costs):

Senior Partner	$275
Partner	$135
Senior Associate	$110
Senior Associate	$105
Junior Associate	$ 75
Paralegal	$ 40

IV. Estimated Tasks and Time Costs
A. Initial Motion, Answer, and Interrogatory Phase

Resulting from the litigation strategy adopted, a substantial amount of time was spent in the first 30 days of our retention preparing an answer, a memorandum, and reply memorandum in support of a motion to dismiss, interrogatories, and a document request. Additional time may be required to prepare for and argue the motion. This phase ended on [date]. Some 300 attorney hours were expended at an approximate cost of $40,000.

B. Pre-Discovery—60–90 days

1. *Overview*   During this time period, it is expected that facts will be elicited from discussions with the client and a review of pertinent documents that will enable further development and refinement of the legal strategy for defending the case. While the primary focus of these efforts will be upon developing the defense against the Sherman Act Section 1 and Robinson-Patman Act claims—in light of the pendency of the motion to dismiss the remaining legal claims—it is recognized that there is considerable overlap in terms of the facts which will have to be explored, *e.g.*, in defense of the Sherman Section 1 and 2 and Clayton Section 3 claims. Therefore, irrespective of the outcome of the motion,

it is anticipated that the basic factual investigation will have been substantially completed during this period.

The Section 1 Claim. In order to prevail in its Section 1 claim [ABC] will be required to prove, initially, that [ABC's] termination was not the result of unilateral conduct on the part of [XYZ]; *i.e.*, that there existed a "contract, combination or conspiracy" among [XYZ Corporation] and one or more of [XYZ's] distributors which resulted in the termination. [ABC] will attempt to prove that [XYZ] terminated [ABC] upon the complaint, and at the instance, of other distributors, thereby transforming [XYZ's] unilateral policy of refusing to deal with distributors handling competing products into a *per se* illegal horizontal group boycott. Alternatively, [ABC] will attempt to prove that [XYZ], through various communications with, and enforcement activities directed at, its distributors, entered into vertical arrangements to be evaluated under the rule of reason. [ABC] will then seek to prove that the effects of the vertical arrangements were anticompetitive, having an adverse impact, *inter alia*, on interbrand competition, and thus warranting condemnation under the rule of reason.

In defense, [XYZ] first can seek to demonstrate that its sales policy was unilaterally adopted and implemented, and that the decision to terminate [ABC] was in furtherance of [XYX's] own business interests, and not those of its other distributors. Even were it possible to conclude that [XYZ's] conduct went beyond purely unilateral announcement of policy, [XYX] can seek to demonstrate that any joint conduct was of a purely vertical nature, was reasonable and pro-competitive in the light of relevant market considerations, and accordingly did not unreasonably restrain trade.

In pursuing the Section 1 defense, there are a number of broad areas into which factual investigation is advisable, including: [ABC]'s historical relationship with [XYZ]; [ABC]'s relationship with other suppliers (especially [W Corp.]) (some of this information will, of course, have to be derived from discovery of [ABC] itself); [ABC]'s significance in its trading area (full information here is also likely to require discovery); the circumstances surrounding [ABC]'s termination; [XYZ's] termination of other distributors—both before and after [ABC]'s termination; the development and carrying out of [XYZ's] sales policy; [XYZ's] relationships with its other distributors over the past five or so years, including communications with such distributors concerning either the sales policy or [ABC]'s termination; [XYZ's] competitors—products sold, distributors available, market shares, etc.; and market definition—product and geographic.

Robinson-Patman Claim. [ABC]'s claims under the Robinson-Patman Act are, at this point, amorphous—a single paragraph in the complaint.

Our outstanding discovery requests seek to elicit more specific information as to the bases, if any, for those claims. In the meanwhile, some 20 interrogatories directed at [XYZ Corporation] seek to elicit a wide range of information from the defendants in support of the claims. It will therefore be appropriate during this time period to begin to investigate pricing and pricing policies in the sale of its [equipment], its related cost and accounting structures and policies, its rebate and quantity discount practices, and the implementation of the foregoing in sales to distributors. Depending upon the results of the investigation, further work can be done to develop appropriate cost justification, meeting competition, or other defenses to possible Robinson-Patman violations.

The potential burden associated with the foregoing is readily apparent, and it will be appropriate to discuss means of minimizing that burden while at the same time developing the necessary information.

2. *Tasks* to be undertaken during this phase include:

a. Commencement of interviews of [XYZ] personnel to identify facts.

b. Commencement of review of documents.

c. Preparation of preliminary fact memorandum.

d. Commencement of preparation of interrogatory answers and objections and preparation for possible discovery motions.

3. *Estimated costs* based on the following time projections:

Senior partner (5 hours); Partner (60 hours); Senior associate (125 hours); Senior associate (50 hours); Junior associate (250 hours); and Paralegal (100 hours)

$50–60,000

C. Document Production, Interrogatory Answer, and Deposition Preparation Phase—90–120 Days

1. *Overview*   Even allowing for the deferral and/or objection to discovery responses based on grounds of general relevance or burden or the pendency of the motion to dismiss, it is anticipated that a substantial volume of documents will be determined to be responsive to [ABC's] outstanding request and, likewise, that a substantial portion of the pending interrogatories ought to be answered. We would also anticipate that there will be matters relating to discovery by both sides which will require negotiation and, given the early dealings with opposing counsel, in all likelihood, assistance from the Court. Finally, it is to be expected that both sides, upon completion of at least substantial responses to interro-

gatories and production of documents, will notice depositions, adequate preparation for which will be required.

2. *Tasks* to be undertaken during this phase include:

a. Completion of assembly and production of documents requested in plaintiff's first document request.

b. Review of documents produced by and interrogatory answers of plaintiff.

c. Preparation of answers and objections to plaintiff's first set of interrogatories.

d. Negotiation with respect to objections to interrogatories and document requests and litigation over discovery disputes.

e. Continuation of fact investigation.

f. Commencement of preparation of outlines for [ABC] witnesses likely to be deposed.

g. Commencement of preparation of [XYZ] witnesses likely to be deposed.

3. *Estimated costs* based on the following projected time:

Senior partner (5 hours); Partner (150 hours); Senior associate (200 hours); Senior associate (50 hours); Junior associate (300 hours); and Paralegal (240 hours)

$80–90,000

D. Deposition Phase, Final Discovery, and Possible Motion Practice—180–240 days

1. *Overview*   Prior to further factual investigation, it is somewhat premature to determine the precise extent of the depositions which the defendants will wish to take beyond key personnel at [ABC]. Certain third-party depositions may be desirable, *e.g.*, to develop information as to the nature and competitiveness of the marketplace in which [XYZ] and its distributors do business. It is likewise difficult to predict the extent to which [ABC] will seek depositions—of [XYZ Corporation] and third parties. Our estimates in this portion of the budget should be viewed, therefore, as particularly tentative.

Additional potential activities for this period are listed below.

2. *Tasks* to be undertaken during this period include:

a. Taking and defending depositions of [ABC] and [XYZ] personnel and possible third-party witnesses. (Time estimates are based on the assumption that [ABC] will take eight depositions of [XYZ] personnel and five third-party depositions and that [XYZ] will take five depositions of [ABC] personnel and two third-party depositions.)

   b. Discovery "clean up" and resolution of remaining discovery
disputes.
   c. Court conferences.
   d. Possible pretrial motions, *e.g.*, for summary judgment as to
some or all claims.
   3. *Estimated costs* based on the following projected time:
Senior partner (5 hours); Partner (240 hours); Senior associate (300
hours); Senior associate (100 hours); Junior associate (400 hours); and
Paralegal (400 hours)

$125–140,000

E. Trial Preparation—60–90 Days

   1. *Tasks* to be undertaken during this period include:
   a. Assembling facts.
   b. Preparation of witnesses.
   c. Submission of trial briefs.
   d. Attendance at Court conferences.
   2. *Estimated costs* based on the following projected time:
Senior partner (20 hours); Partner (200 hours); Senior associate (200
hours); Senior associate (75 hours); Junior associate (300 hours); and
Paralegal (300 hours)

$95–105,000

F. Trial—8–12 Days

   1. An 8–12 day jury trial is assumed.
   2. *Estimated costs* based on the following projected time:
Senior partner (20 hours); Partner (100 hours); Senior associate (100
hours); Senior associate (50 hours); Junior associate (100 hours); and
Paralegal (100 hours)

$45–55,000

V. Estimated Disbursements

   A. This estimate is based on a review of past cases. It assumes some,
but not extensive, travel with all of it being in the northeast. The estimates
cover the time parameters referred to above.
   B. *Estimates*

Travel	$10,000
Transcripts	15,000
Xerox	20,000
Nonlegal overtime	7,000
Miscellaneous	20,000
	$72,000

Proposed Preliminary Budget for [ABC Corporation] v. [XYZ Corporation]			
Phase	Duration	Estimated Total Cost	Estimated Average Cost per Month
Initial Motion, Answer, and Interrogatory Responses	30 Days	$ 40,000	—
Pre-Discovery	60–90 Days	40–60,000	$20–30,000
Document Production, Interrogatory Answer, and Deposition Preparation	90–120 Days	80–90,000	20–30,000
Depositions, Final Discovery, Motion Practice	180–240 Days	125–140,000	15–20,000
Trial Preparation	60–90 Days	95–105,000	30–50,000
Trial	8–12 Days	45–55,000	
Estimated Total Time	14–19 Mos.	$435,000–500,000	—
Disbursements		$ 72,000	

APPENDIX F

The Corporate Policy Statement (ADR Pledge)

The following paragraph is the Corporate Policy Statement (or ADR Pledge, as it was originally known). Following it is a list of almost 100 companies that had, through their CEOs, subscribed to the pledge by March 1985.

THE ALTERNATIVE DISPUTE RESOLUTION PLEDGE

We recognize that for many business disputes there is a less expensive, more effective method of resolution than the traditional lawsuit. Alternative dispute resolution (ADR) techniques involve collaborative techniques which often can spare businesses the high cost and wear and tear of litigation.

In recognition of the foregoing, we subscribe to the following statement of principle. In the event of a business dispute between our corporation and another corporation which has made or will then make a similar statement, we are prepared to explore, with that other party, resolution of the dispute through negotiation or ADR techniques, before resorting to full-scale litigation. If either party believes that the dispute is not suitable for ADR techniques, or if such techniques do not produce results satisfactory to the disputants, either party may proceed with litigation.

X CORPORATION

_____

Chief Executive Officer

_____

Chief Legal Officer

_____

Date

SUBSCRIBERS TO CORPORATE POLICY STATEMENT ON ADR*

Abbott Laboratories
Aetna Life & Casualty
Air Products and Chemicals, Inc.
Allen-Bradley Company
Aluminum Company of America
American Can Company
American Cyanamid Company
American Express Company
American Hoechst Corporation
American Telephone & Telegraph
ASARCO Incorporated
BankAmerica Corporation
Bethlehem Steel Corporation
Borden, Inc.
Borg-Warner Corporation
Bristol-Myers Company
Brown & Root, Inc.
Burlington Industries, Inc.
Caschem, Inc.
Celanese Corporation
The Chase Manhattan Corporation
Chevron Corporation
Chrysler Corporation
CIGNA Corporation
Columbia Nitrogen Corp./NIPRO, Inc.
Conoco, Inc.
Consumers Power Company
Continental Baking Company, Inc.
Control Data Corporation
Crum & Forster
Deere & Company
Dennison Manufacturing Company
Digital Equipment Corporation
E. I. Du Pont de Nemours and Company
Eaton Corporation
Eli Lilly and Company
Federal-Mogul Corporation
Ferro Corporation
FMC Corporation
Ford Motor Company

General Alum & Chemical Corporation
General Mills, Inc.
Georgia-Pacific Corporation
The Goodyear Tire & Rubber Company
Great Lakes Chemical Corporation
Grolier Inc.
GTE Corporation
Heublein, Inc.
Honeywell, Inc.
Household International
ICI Americas Inc.
ITT Corporation
Kaiser Aluminum & Chemical Corp.
Kentucky Fried Chicken Corp.
Mallinckrodt, Inc.
McDonnell Douglas Corporation
McKesson Corporation
The Mead Corporation
Minnesota Mining & Manufacturing Co. (3M)
Monsanto Company
Mooney Chemicals, Inc.
National Starch & Chemical Corp.
Northrop Corporation
Olin Corporation
Owens-Illinois, Inc.
Parker-Hannifin Corporation
Peat Marwick
J. C. Penney Company, Inc.
Pfizer, Inc.
Phillips Petroleum Company
PPG Industries
The Prudential Insurance Co. of North America
Reichhold Chemicals, Inc.
Rexnord, Inc.
R. J. Reynolds Industries, Inc.
Rockwell International Corp.
Rohm and Haas Company
Sears, Roebuck and Company

* Subscription applies to parent company and domestic subsidiaries; list is as of March 21, 1985. Total: 96.

Shaklee Corporation
Siemens Capital Corporation
Sun Company, Inc.
Transamerica Corporation
The Travelers Companies
TRW Inc.
Union Carbide Corporation
Union Oil Company of California
Union Pacific Corporation
Uniroyal, Inc.

United Parcel Service of America,
   Inc.
Wells Fargo & Company
Westinghouse Electric Corporation
Whirlpool Corporation
A. L. Williams Corporation
Wisconsin Electric Power Company
Witco Chemical Corporation
Xerox Corporation

FURTHER READING

The Mini-Trial Workbook, ed. by the CPR Legal Program, 1985.

This looseleaf workbook is the most complete compendium of information on the minitrial in print. It includes a wealth of forms.

Corporate Dispute Management, by the Center for Public Resources, Matthew Bender & Co., 1982.

A collection of readings covering the gamut of ADR processes, cases, and preventive practices, covering a variety of substantive areas, including intercorporate disputes, environmental disputes, employee disputes, and others.

The Litigious Society, by Jethro K. Lieberman, Basic Books, 1983.

The first comprehensive look at the phenomenon of litigation in the United States and an assessment of its impact in a variety of industries and professions.

The Role of Courts in American Society, principal editor, Jethro K. Lieberman, for the Council on the Role of Courts, West Publishing Co., 1984.

An analysis of the functions that courts perform, together with an extensive collection of statistical data on the numbers and types of lawsuits in the federal and state court systems.

Alternatives to the High Cost of Litigation, a monthly newsletter, featuring news and case studies on ADR. Published by the Center for Public Resources, 680 Fifth Avenue, New York, N.Y. 10019.

Getting to Yes, by Roger Fisher and William Ury, Penguin Books, 1983.

The classic statement of the negotiation technique based on interests rather than positions.

Mediation, by Jay Folberg and Alison Taylor, Jossey-Bass, 1984.

A guide to the technique and practice of mediation in contemporary disputes.

Justice Without Law? by Jerold S. Auerbach, Oxford University Press, 1983.

A concise history of a variety of ADR movements in our nation's past.

INDEX

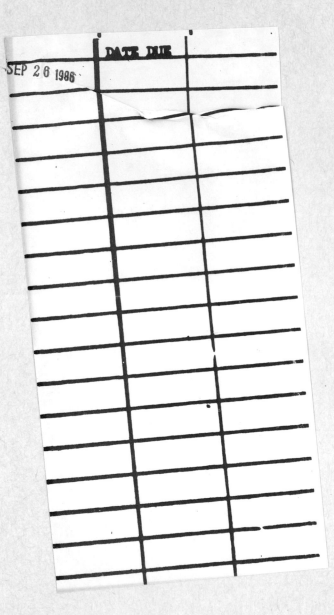